Stanislavsky's Use of Improvisation

"Theatre history and contemporary practice coexist in illuminating ways in Aquilina's latest very valuable contribution to Stanislavsky studies. Spanning his entire career from amateur actor to international legend, this ingenious book reveals an improvisational through-line to Stanislavsky's practice which helps cohere a diverse and complex career, all the more so with the inclusion of tried and tested practical exercises to conclude each section."
—Prof. Jonathan Pitches, *School of Performance and Cultural Industries, University of Leeds*

"*Stanislavsky's Use of Improvisation* is an invaluable investigation into this highly relevant aspect of Stanislavsky's acting system. With a chronological overview referencing lesser-known productions, the conclusion offers the author's unique process of autoethnographic research as a guide to young scholars."
—Bella Merlin, *University of California, Riverside*

Stefan Aquilina

Stanislavsky's Use of Improvisation

Stefan Aquilina
University of Malta
Msida, Malta

ISBN 978-3-031-84766-0   ISBN 978-3-031-84767-7   (eBook)
https://doi.org/10.1007/978-3-031-84767-7

© The Editor(s) (if applicable) and The Author(s), under exclusive license to Springer Nature Switzerland AG 2025

This work is subject to copyright. All rights are solely and exclusively licensed by the Publisher, whether the whole or part of the material is concerned, specifically the rights of translation, reprinting, reuse of illustrations, recitation, broadcasting, reproduction on microfilms or in any other physical way, and transmission or information storage and retrieval, electronic adaptation, computer software, or by similar or dissimilar methodology now known or hereafter developed.
The use of general descriptive names, registered names, trademarks, service marks, etc. in this publication does not imply, even in the absence of a specific statement, that such names are exempt from the relevant protective laws and regulations and therefore free for general use.
The publisher, the authors and the editors are safe to assume that the advice and information in this book are believed to be true and accurate at the date of publication. Neither the publisher nor the authors or the editors give a warranty, expressed or implied, with respect to the material contained herein or for any errors or omissions that may have been made. The publisher remains neutral with regard to jurisdictional claims in published maps and institutional affiliations.

Cover illustration: Maram_shutterstock.com

This Palgrave Macmillan imprint is published by the registered company Springer Nature Switzerland AG
The registered company address is: Gewerbestrasse 11, 6330 Cham, Switzerland

If disposing of this product, please recycle the paper.

To my family

Acknowledgements I remain indebted to the support that different people offered me, each in their own particular way, during the gestation of this book.

My first thanks go to Eileen Srebernik, Senior Editor of Literature, Theatre, and Performance at Palgrave Macmillan, who immediately saw potential in the project and who was supportive throughout, not to mention highly efficient and responsive. Many thanks also go to the two anonymous reviewers, who offered constructive feedback on the first draft of the manuscript and whose suggestions genuinely improved my work.

I am very proud to be part of the academic body of the University of Malta, which has generously supported my research (and that of many others) through timely sabbaticals and other research resources. Colleagues at the Department of Theatre Studies – Frank Camilleri, Marco Galea, Vicki Ann Cremona, and Mario Frendo – have also been outstanding in their support, advice, and humour. On the international scene, my thanks go to my 'Stanislavsky family', scholars like Jonathan Pitches, Paul Fryer, Bella Merlin, Benjamin Askew, Dassia N. Posner, Julian Jones, Joelle Ré Arp-Dunham, Sharon Marie Carnicke, Maria Shevtsova, Laurence Senelick, Michaela Antoniou, Marie-Christine Autant-Mathieu, Alisa Ballard Lin, and many others who have contributed to create the rich and dynamic field of Stanislavsky studies. I would also like to thank Natalia Fedorova for her help with translation.

This book has been largely conceived during my annual trip at the Isle of Mull, a truly special place where my writing seems to flow so much more easily. My thanks go to the people of Mull who make the island so unique and inspiring.

Finally, and as always, this book is dedicated to my family, to Yulia, Matthew, Daniel, and Alexander for their unending love and support.

Competing Interests The author has no competing interests to declare that are relevant to the content of this manuscript.

Contents

1	Introduction	1
	References	5
2	First Phase: The 1880s and Stanislavsky's Amateur Years	7
	References	15
3	Second Phase: 1903–08, Placing Improvisation in the Production Process	17
	References	33
4	Third Phase: 1912–16, The First Studio and Stanislavsky's Offshoots	35
	References	51
5	Fourth Phase: 1924–28 and Stanislavsky's Final Legacies of the 1930s	53
	References	67
6	Conclusion	69
	References	78
	Index	81

About the Author

Stefan Aquilina is Associate Professor of Theatre Studies at the University of Malta, Co-Director of the Stanislavsky Research Centre, and Editor-in-Chief of the journal *Stanislavski Studies*. His research focuses on modern theatre, especially Stanislavsky and Meyerhold, but has wider interest in the transmission of embodied practice, amateur theatre, devised performance, and reflective teaching. Aquilina's book publications include *Stanislavsky in the World: The System and its Transformations Across Continents* (Bloomsbury, 2017) and *The Routledge Companion to Vsevolod Meyerhold* (Routledge, 2023), both co-edited with Jonathan Pitches, as well as *Modern Theatre in Russia* (sole author, Bloomsbury, 2020) and *Stanislavsky and Pedagogy* (editor, Routledge, 2023). His current book project is a monograph-length study titled *Performing Academia: Building a Successful University Career* (contracted to Bloomsbury).

CHAPTER 1

Introduction

Abstract The Introduction of the book *Stanislavsky's Use of Improvisation* refers to *An Actor's Work* and uses the students' demonstrations at the beginning of that book to make the foundational point that improvisation does not imply doing unplanned things on stage but rather the potential, following serious preparation, for the actor to find spontaneity in performance. The four Phases around which the narrative is framed are also introduced.

Keywords Spontaneity · Experiencing · Historiography · Periodization · Improvisation

To open *An Actor's Work*, his seminal book on acting, Konstantin Stanislavsky described a group of students tasked with presenting a number of short scenes to their teacher, Arkady Tortsov, for his feedback and criticism. Two key presentations were given by Konstantin (Kostya) Nazvanov, the narrator of the fictitious diary, and Pavel (Pasha) Shustov. The two presentations were very different from each other, but Stanislavsky managed to bring the two together to launch a key discussion about improvisation. Pasha's presentation appeared finished and complete. He planned each and every moment and executed the whole piece with clinical precision, even if not without artistry. In fact,

© The Author(s), under exclusive license to Springer Nature Switzerland AG 2025
S. Aquilina, *Stanislavsky's Use of Improvisation*,
https://doi.org/10.1007/978-3-031-84767-7_1

in his feedback Tortsov remarked that in Pasha's 'playing there was a coldness which led me to suspect that his performance was fixed once and for all, leaving no room for improvisation, thus denying freshness and spontaneity' (Stanislavski, 2008: 23). Kostya's presentation, though marred by a series of naïve clichés, did show isolated moments when he managed to tap into the art of experiencing, i.e. creative moments when the actor is at one with the role. These moments, 'unexpectedly rise to great artistic heights which stun the audience. The actor experiences or creates on inspiration, in a kind of *improvisation*' (21; emphasis added). This understanding of improvisation does not mean that the actor carries out unplanned things on stage, that he invents on the spur of the moment—Kostya had already tried this in a rehearsal with dire consequences (9). It rather means that the actor, following serious preparation, manages to find the creative space necessary to live through the role every night as if it is being played for the first time. The role, in other words, is experienced anew: 'In our kind of acting, which means experiencing every moment in the role, that experiencing must be felt anew and physically embodied anew' (23).

Stanislavsky's career can be read as a search for the ideal conditions that stimulate this state of improvisation. It is a reading attempted by this short book, which charts Stanislavsky's use of improvisation as it developed throughout his career. For the sake of organising the material, I identify four main phases of work, namely:

- First Phase: The 1880s and Stanislavsky's Amateur Years
- Second Phase: 1903–08, Placing Improvisation in the Production Process
- Third Phase: 1912–16, The First Studio and Stanislavsky's Offshoots
- Fourth Phase: 1924–28 and Stanislavsky's Final Legacies of the 1930s

My approach is therefore a linear one, fully aware that the work of any practitioner or even of theatre histories in general rarely fits into such neat categorisation or periodization (Aquilina, 2020: 195–98). Still, the identification of these phases allows me to organise the material in what I feel is an accessible manner, and as the reader will note I often cross-refer materials or examples across the different phases. My identification of these phases is based on a balance between, on the one hand, several instances in Stanislavsky's work which have been rather side-lined in contemporary scholarship (e.g. his amateur years, the production of *Ivan Mironich* and *Artists and Admirers*, notes to the 1907–08 season, rehearsal processes in the mid-1920s) and, on the other, more familiar examples which however benefit when reappraised from the point of view of improvisation (the creation of a mise-en-scène, the First Studio, and his final legacies). The diversity of the work that Stanislavsky carried out—hardly surprising given that these phases extend over five decades—shows that improvisation is a highly mutable practice that adapts to a broad range of theatre concerns, from directing to acting, teaching, and even experimentation and research. It is this adaptability that ultimately made improvisation a recurrent concern for Stanislavsky.

The choice of these phases and the examples they feature is ultimately dictated by those instances where I noted Stanislavsky's use of improvisation to be particularly prominent. They are, therefore, at least partly subjective. As in all historical research, these phases and their narratives are far from exhaustive, and I am sure any other scholar attempting a similar study would identify alternative milestones, case-studies, or even conclusions. As Thomas Postlewait (2009: 6) says, 'the plurality of interpretations [in historical study is] [...] an incontestable fact, [one] which the historian must accept'. Such pluralities are, in my opinion, where the beauty of theatre histories and historiography lies, and it is a plurality and difference that I am always keen to celebrate and which continues to draw me towards projects of this kind.

The methodology that I adopt in this book can be explained as follows. When developing Active Analysis, his final, improvisation-heavy, rehearsal approach, Stanislavsky urged his actors to always align themselves to their 'here, today, now', and to use that as a way into their roles. This acting concern for the 'here, today, now' seeped into the way that I approached this project which, in other words, is also strongly informed by where I stand 'here, today, now' in my own trajectory as a (mid-career) scholar engaged in the fields of theatre and performance. I have often described myself, half-jokingly but not too far away from the mark, as a 'good old-fashioned theatre historian'. In fact, I was always perfectly at home working in archives and libraries, consulting primary sources and evaluating secondary ones, writing and editing historical narratives, and so on. However, this core historical interest is now allied to practical work and teaching, an aspect of my work which has not only been increasing, but which I have found myself revaluating in the wake of the COVID-19 pandemic. My 'here, today, now' still engages with theatre histories, but less in a 'pure' or 'unalloyed' way as I continue to look into ways of connecting history-based research with practical endeavour like actor training, workshop settings, and embodied and performance work—Gilli Bush-Bailey and Jackie Bratton's articulation of a 'practice-based research in theatre history [...] [i.e. of] [w]orking historically through practice' was a crucial reference point here (Bush-Bailey & Bratton, 2012: 98).

My 'here, today, now' was also irrevocably shaped by a 4 years-term as the Director of the School of Performing Arts of the University of Malta (2019–23). The highlight for me during this term was overseeing a considerable increase in staff recruitment who, once appointed, required training and support, especially because many were still in the early and formative years of their career. I enjoyed giving this training, and still do, which means that in my day-to-day work I now find myself juggling the provision of academic formation with history-based research, practical classes in actor training and performance-making, more straightforward lecture-based teaching, editing a journal, and carrying out service.

It seemed only logical for me to try and maximise my time and resources by treating these various aspects of work not in isolation but as a network of academic tasks that support and even enable each other. In fact, this current volume is informed by such a spread of academic work. Historical-study certainly remains at its core, but I am also including a number of exercises and suggestions for practice. The aim of these exercises is to translate some of the historical ideas into practical material that is useful in a classroom, studio, or rehearsal situation. The exercises can also be read as my attempt to develop a more experiential understanding of the historical material presented. No previous experience is necessary to carry out these exercises, as the emphasis is on exploration rather than proficiency or skill. Some research perspectives arising from this study on Stanislavsky and improvisation then conclude the book. The impulse for this final part of the book harks back to the academic formation that I am engaging in. My intention is to draw out some guidelines that could be used by others to assist them in their own projects and I humbly offer these guidelines as some examples of (hopefully) good academic practice. It is my hope that theatre researchers, especially early career researchers who might still be finding their feet in the discipline, may find these guidelines helpful. I can guarantee only one thing: they have been thoroughly tried and tested. Now, over to Stanislavsky and his use of improvisation.

References

Aquilina, S. (2020) Teaching Stanislavsky: Periodization and the formation of theatre Canons. *Stanislavski Studies, 8*(2), 193–208.

Bush-Bailey, G., & Bratton, J. (2012). Case-study 2: Memory, absence and agency: an approach to practice-based research in theatre history. In B. Kershaw & H. Nicholson (Eds.), *Research methods in theatre and performance* (pp. 98–108). Edinburgh University Press.

Postlewait, T. (2009). *The Cambridge introduction to theatre historiography*. Cambridge University Press.

Stanislavski, K. (2008). *An actor's work* (J. Benedetti, Trans.). Routledge.

CHAPTER 2

First Phase: The 1880s and Stanislavsky's Amateur Years

Abstract This chapter reviews Stanislavsky's amateur years from the point of view of improvisation. While his main acting method at the time involved the imitation of the mannerisms of famous actors, an argument is made that Stanislavsky also appreciated the more developed action-based behaviours with which these actors gave depth to their characters. Evidence shows that Stanislavsky referred to these 'mini scenes' as 'improvisations' through which actors carved a creative space from both the text and the type. Therefore, improvisation in the context of late nineteenth-century theatre and Stanislavsky's first acting methods is used as a term to describe stage behaviour that (i) is not prescribed by the text (ii) arises from the actor (iii) serves as a tool for characterisation and (iv) engages the audience with its vividness and unexpectedness.

Keywords Amateurism · Imitation · Nineteenth-century theatre · Types/emploi · Improvisation

It is a well-known fact that Stanislavsky's first acting method involved copying the stage behaviour of other actors. This meant close observation of the mannerisms and voice of a particular actor. The actor Nikolai Musil, who had a long association with the Maly Theatre, was Stanislavsky's first model. In fact, it was Musil whom Stanislavsky copied when preparing for his stage debut in the play *A Cup of Tea* (September 1877):

> It was quite primitive. All I wanted was to be like my favourite actor, Nikolai Musil, who played simpletons. I wanted to have his voice and his manner. They were what I liked best in this beautiful actor, now dead. And so all I did was work on his external tricks, and develop a hoarse voice. I wanted to be an exact copy. [...] I knew every moment, move, intonation, gesture, facial expression of my favourite actor. [...] [A]ll that remained for me was to repeat something that had already been done and blindly copy the original. I felt wonderful, free and self-assured onstage. (Stanislavski, 2008a: 35–36)

As Maria Ignatieva (2013: 15) says, '[c]opying his favourite actors had always given [Stanislavsky] a shot of confidence'. It proved to be a relatively lasting method. Three years later, Stanislavsky still remarked that while he had stopped copying Musil's voice, he had 'retained his manners' (Stanislavskii, 1993: 192).[1] Other actors he copied included Bouldin, 'a student at the conservatoire, [even if] nothing came out of it' and, more successfully, '[Viktor] Rodon, a little in his voice' (194).[2] Another, now long-forgotten actor on whom Stanislavsky modelled some of his acting was Chernov.[3] More enduring models included some leading actors of the Imperial Theatres, like Aleksandr Lensky[4] and Prov Sadovski. On the latter, Stanislavsky remarked as follows:

> [A]s was my habit then, I started to imitate Sadovski, a famous actor from the Imperial theatres.[5] I worked on this absurd walk with his pigeon toes, his shortsightedness, clumsy hands, his habit of tugging at the hairs in his straggly beard, of adjusting his glasses and the long forelocks that covered them. (Stanislavski, 2008a: 44)

Such manners and habits easily stand out in performance. Their impression on a young actor like Stanislavsky who lacked a solid technique and even a general know-how-to-do is clear and to a certain extent understandable. Stanislavsky wanted to act, and wanted to act well; without any training, he resorted to the imitation of the actors he looked up to. Some creativity was possible when Stanislavsky combined together elements from different actors, as he did in January 1884 when performing in a play called *Prank*. In this performance he copied Lensky's acting over which he superimposed Chernov's singing (Stanislavskii, 1993: 199).

However, a closer look at Stanislavsky's diary entries found in his *Sobranie Sochinenii* [Collected Works, both editions] evidences how his study of actors, especially those of the Maly, went beyond the crude imitation of outer mannerisms. Stanislavsky's attention was also drawn to how a number of actors, including Musil, handled physical, action-based behaviour onstage. This behaviour is different from simple mannerisms. Mannerisms are the habitual behavioural traits synonymous with a particular actor rather than with a specific stage character (e.g. Musil's hoarse voice). They manifest the personality of the actor more than the uniqueness of a character and, in fact, an actor's mannerisms tend to repeat themselves across a number of roles. In contrast to mannerisms, the stage behaviour that impressed Stanislavsky reads as a veritable physical score attached to a particular moment of performance, a contained micro scene within the larger, macro event taking place on the stage. More than an actor's indulgence, these micro scenes allow the actor to portray the complexities and specific nuances of a role. The following is a key example Stanislavsky observed in Musil. The diary entry relates to a performance of Aleksandr Ostrovsky's play *The Marriage of Balzaminov*, staged at the Maly on the 6 February 1885:

> In the first act there is a scene where Balzaminov's mother and the matchmaker strongly reproach the young groom [played by Musil]. He, accustomed to such family scenes, initially remains indifferent to what the women say. He walks around the room with his hands in the pockets, catching flies on the walls. Musil, in a very funny and believable way, targets an imaginary fly and, having missed, follows the insect with his eyes for a long time. When he managed to catch the fly, he took special pleasure in swatting it against the floor. It all came out very nicely for him, since there was not the slightest bit of exaggeration.
> However, the scolding of the two women became increasingly stronger, so that Balzaminov was forced to object. His answers became more and more rude. Despite this, he soon calmed down to the point that he again began catching flies. He caught one, kept it in his fist, and tried to catch it with two fingers in order to remove its wings. (Stanislavskii, 1958: 74–75).[6]

Stanislavsky realised that this moment of performance contained traces of an acting technique where the actor delivers an action-based micro scene not only to connect with the character but also to 'complete' the scene. The commentary to Stanislavsky's diaries refer several times to these micro scenes as 'improvisations'. N. N. Chushkin, for example, says that in the 1880s Stanislavsky was 'especially interested in everyday characterisation, the skill of impersonation, and the actor's ability to enrich the role by introducing improvisational vivid life details' (in Stanislavskii, 1958: 7). 'Improvisation' is the term Stanislavsky himself was still using years later to describe these action-based contributions from the actor. This is evident in a passage from *An Actor's Work* where he uses Tortsov's voice to recount the impact of Eleonora Duse's acting:

> When Eleonora Duse came to Moscow for the first time I saw her in *La Dame aux Camélias*. There was a long pause in which she wrote a letter to Armand. I can remember that famous improvisation not 'in general' but in all its constituent moments. They have stuck in my memory with unusual clarity, brilliance, in all their perfection: I loved that improvisation as a whole and in its parts, as one loves a magnificent example of the goldsmith's art. (Stanislavski, 2008b: 622)

Two other instances from Stanislavsky's diary entries shed further light on the nature of these improvisational contributions. The first relates to the actor Forcatti (Viktor Lyudrigovich, 1846–1906), a popular provincial actor and later an entrepreneur. In a performance of the play *Trouble has Come—Open the Gate* or *Where the Fuss Caught Fire*,[7] '[i]t is possible that, by way of improvisation, [Forcatti] introduced details not indicated in the text of the play' (Chushkin in Stanislavskii, 1958: 550). It is this addition of details 'not indicated in the text' that seems to qualify this stage behaviour as an 'improvisation'. In this sense, improvisation becomes a space for the actor to express his own interpretation of the character and creative autonomy—a recurring point in this book. Forcatti's physical details included contemplating the tips of his leather shoes; taking out a handkerchief 'to brush off what was amusing him so much'; showing interest in the dress of his listener, on whom he fixes his gaze; looking at his watch, 'figuring out something from it'; and 'repeating the same phrase [from the text] as if helping himself with gestures'. Finally, he fell completely silent, and 'continued looking at his watch with the same attention and serious look'. This is performance material rooted in action-based behaviour that strikes one for its naturalness rather than for any actorial stock-in-trade. As a young actor, Stanislavsky was impressed by its spontaneity and lightness. It captivated the attention of the audience in what Stanislavsky describes as an otherwise rather uninspiring scene. He 'could not help but write it down' (Stanislavskii, 1958: 73–74).

Another diary entry refers to the actor Ivan Kiselevsky (1839–98), another talented provincial actor who also performed at the Korsh and the Alexandrinsky. Kiselevsky 'had a gift for stage improvisation. Playing in clichéd, craft plays, he skilfully enriched the role, introducing a number of vivid, life-like details not provided by the author' (Chushkin in Stanislavskii, 1958: 550).[8] The use of the term improvisation to refer to these actorial additions as a way of augmenting a text is to be noted again. Acting in the second part of the nineteenth century was rooted in the portrayal of conventional types like the simpleton, military man, merchant, young lovers, peasant, doting father, and others. Also known as emploi, each type had its own set of behavioural traits, which the actor learned, and which the audience grew 'familiar with [...], beginning to expect it at every performance, regardless of the play' (Merlin, 2003: 7).[9] Action-based, 'improvised additions' like Kiselevsky's (and Forcatti's and Musil's) helped actors to exert their creative independence from the type as well as from the text.[10] They are contributions from the actor that improve the production of weak texts, as was the case in Forcatti's example, a concern which Stanislavsky would also exhibit in his work as an actor and later on as a director (Stanislavski, 2008a: 131).[11]

The combination of Forcatti and Kiselevsky was, for Stanislavsky, quite a sight to behold. A performance of the two together is documented in a diary entry dated 25 February 1885.[12] It is again worth quoting at length from this entry:

> Kiselevsky and Forcatti are present on stage for almost half the scene but without saying a word. To keep themselves busy, they sit at the back of the stage and seem to talk about something in a business-like manner. Of course, they maintain gestures appropriate to the role. It is clear that Kiselevsky is bragging; every now and then you notice that he seems to be saying to Forcatti: 'What, sir?...How, sir, you don't believe...no?' He even leans his whole body towards him for greater persuasiveness. He gets more and more excited by the minute.
> Finally, Kiselevsky reaches the extreme limit, and quickly jumps up from the chair. He takes a few steps to the side and impulsively puts his hands in both pockets...He seems to be outraged by some stupid objection of Forcatti and answers annoyingly: 'Yes...what are you...no, no, not at all.' He even says a few words loudly, without paying attention to the other artists on stage: 'Shhh...shhh...what are you saying...I...I 've seen it myself with my own eyes'. Then he continues quietly, and quickly sits down in his original place. Their dispute subsides; they sit quietly for a while, and

begin to tell each other funny jokes, jump up from their chairs, explain something with gestures and occasionally utter loudly some fragmentary phrases. Such a performance is extremely effective only if done truthfully. (Stanislavskii, 1958: 75–76)

What qualifies this stage business as an 'improvisation' is that it is not mentioned in the text but arises from the actors' imaginative reaction to a specific performance moment. If a performance is dragging a piece of action-based behaviour is promptly inserted by the actor(s) in a manner that, in contrast with the fixity of a text, takes the audience by surprise. The working conditions of the actors facilitated these momentary additions. Actors worked together for considerable lengthy periods, such as the members of the Maly theatre for instance, and often on a rather restricted range of roles. This familiarity sensitised the actors to each other's talents, quirks, routines, and practices.

These entries from Stanislavsky's diaries perhaps do show his initial naivety as an actor; in 1885, when he watched Kiselevsky and Forcatti, Stanislavsky was, after all, only twenty-two years old. In contrast to the rigidity of the written word in a text, the actor's work appeared spontaneous and alive. He prepared himself for the author's text by reading, wherever possible, the play before the performance, but in comparison the acting took him much more by surprise, especially given the fact that he was observing talented actors with a unique creative personality. In the context of Stanislavsky's first acting methods, improvisation is therefore used as a term to describe stage behaviour that (i) is not prescribed by the text (ii) arises from the actor (iii) serves as a tool for characterisation and (iv) engages the audience with its vividness and unexpectedness. That this action-based behaviour emerges in unexpected moments is, perhaps, the strongest qualification that Stanislavsky gave it as an improvised piece of theatre. Moreover, the fact that performances in the nineteenth century were typically put on after only a few rehearsals makes me think that while the general framework of the action-based physical behaviour was prepared (e.g. Forcatti would know of his stage business with the shoes, handkerchief, and watch), its placement within the broader scene and overall duration was a more spontaneous endeavour which the actor realised in the here and now of performance.[13]

Another feature that underscores these improvisations is their realistic nature, with their contents being sourced directly from everyday life and behaviour. Improvisation and everyday life are brought closer together

2 FIRST PHASE: THE 1880S AND STANISLAVSKY'S AMATEUR ... 13

by Stanislavsky's rehearsal practice at the Alekseev Circle[14] which saw the actors living throughout the day not as themselves but as the characters 'within the circumstances of [a] play' (Stanislavski, 2008a: 43; see also 55). This allowed the actors to develop a deeper engagement with the character, certainly deeper than if they had simply imitated another actor's mannerisms. Stanislavsky noted the difficulty of these experiments because the 'actors [had to become] [...] the authors of one new improvisation after another' (44). The performances of *The Practical Man* and *Javotta* were prepared in this manner. Other improvisations were more akin to 'inventing on the spot'. These were the pranks which Stanislavsky and others again played in their life, like dressing up as penniless drunks. They gauged the success of these 'performances' from the reactions of the passers-by (Stanislavski, 2008a: 39–40). It is a practice that would find a place even in Stanislavsky's later, more mature, phases.

Improvising micro scenes
- Choose a scene in a play where your character is largely silent and seemingly not contributing much to the scene. The part when the stage hands set up the stage for Treplev's play in the opening scene of *The Seagull* comes to mind, even if in the stage directions the workmen are behind the curtain and therefore unseen. Another example is the scene in *Three Sisters* when Olga and Irina are reminiscing about Moscow while Masha remains essentially silent and detached.
- Improvise a score of action-based physical behaviour, a micro scene, with the sole purpose of manifesting a particular trait of your character. Be specific about this trait. It could be: a reaction, like anger or surprise, to something that happens on the stage; boredom or lack of interest in what is happening to the other characters; fixation with a seemingly mundane activity; etc.
- It is important that the actions are your own composition as an actor and that they are not derived from the playwright's stage directions. If need be, delete or erase these directions so as to facilitate your own engagement with the character.
- How does this improvisation relate to the macro scene as a whole? Does it connect with it? Does your contribution overshadow the main direction of the scene?
- Repeat the exercise but give more attention to how your action-based behaviour fits within the broader scene. What changes? Does

> the improvisation help to unravel both the character and the scene? How is the integration of the micro scene within the larger scene facilitated?
> - Repeat the exercise. Make sure that your actions are defined with some clarity and that you feel secure in the general outline of actions that you want to perform: use Musil's score with the flies as an example, or even Forcatti's work with the objects. Keep the score, but experiment with repetition, duration, intensity, rhythm, magnitude, direction, and other action-related dynamics. Explore, through improvisation, how the dynamics of the score change when it is applied to different scenes.

Notes

1. This observation relates to the role of August Karlovich Fish, which Stanislavsky played in the vaudeville *A and F*. The performance date is 3 August 1880 (Stanislavskii, 1993: 192).
2. The two performances in question are, respectively, Molière's *Le Mariage Forcé*, in which Stanislavsky played the part of Pancras the philosopher, and *Love Potion*, an opera-vaudeville in two acts in which he played the part of Laverger the barber. Both plays were presented on the 24 July 1882 at Liubimovka (Stanislavskii, 1993: 194).
3. In *Javotta*, an operetta in two acts (28 April 1883). Stanislavsky played the role of Nick, a thief. No further details on Chernov are given (Stanislavskii, 1993: 196).
4. In *A Special Kind of Misfortune*, a one-act comedy in which Stanislavsky played the part of Vladimir Nilov, a doctor (28 April 1883). Stanislavsky says that he was particularly successful in this part, and the audience called him a number of times (Stanislavskii, 1993: 196).
5. The play in question was *Artist and Admirers*, where Stanislavsky played the role of the student Melusov (Stanislavski, 2008a: 44). Stanislavsky also imitated Sadovski when performing in *The Practical Man*, a comedy in 4 acts written by Diachenko. Stanislavsky here played the part of Pokrovtsev, a secretary. The play was performed on the 24 August 1883. His sister Zinaida played the

part of Verocka so well that she was 'unrecognisable. She promises to be a wonderful actress for dramatic roles. So far she is diligently copying Ermolova, but who is not guilty of this?' (Stanislavskii, 1993: 197).

6. Translation consultant Natalia Fedorova.
7. From the notes it is unclear which play it was.
8. The notes in volume 5 of Stanislavsky's *Sobranie Sochinenii* (1958) are written by N. N. Chushkin with the participation of G. V. Christie and S. V. Melik-Zakharov. It is impossible to see who exactly wrote what, which is why in the citation I refer only to Chushkin.
9. The actor Vasily Toporkov gives evidence of the use of these types as late as the 1920s. In fact, it was his main method of work before meeting Stanislavsky and joining the Moscow Art Theatre (Toporkov, 1998: 41).
10. In the notes Chushkin refers a number of times to verbal improvisations from the actors studied by Stanislavsky. These are utterances which Stanislavsky noted in his diaries and which were absent in the play-text. For example, see Stanislavskii (1958: 550, notes 4 and 5).
11. 'As was his custom, [Stanislavsky] did not treat the texts with any particular piety, often editing and "improving" them to fit the needs of the performers' (Ignatieva, 2013: 14).
12. Stanislavsky fails to record the title of the performance.
13. '[W]ith only two rehearsals one could give so many more premières', Nikolai Gorchakov (1957: 9) says, which undoubtedly pleased the theatre entrepreneurs.
14. The Alekseev Circle was the theatre group revolving around Stanislavsky's family. Its members included his sisters, brothers, cousins, and friends.

References

Gorchakov, N. A. (1957) *The theater in soviet Russia* (E. Lehrman, Trans.). Columbia University Press.

Ignatieva, M. (2013). Stanislavsky as Amateur: The Alekseev circle. In A. White (Ed.), *The Routledge companion to Stanislavsky* (pp. 13–40). Routledge.

Merlin, B. (2003). *Konstantin Stanislavsky*. Routledge.

Stanislavski, K. (2008a) *My life in art* (J. Benedetti, Trans.). Routledge.
Stanislavski, K. (2008b) *An actor's work* (J. Benedetti, Trans.). Routledge.
Stanislavskii, K. (1958). *Sobranie Sochinenii Tom 5* [Collected Works in 8 Volumes, Volume 5]. Iskusstvo.
Stanislavskii K. (1993). *Sobranie Sochinenii Tom 5.1* [Collected Works in 9 volumes, Volume 5.1]. Iskusstvo.
Toporkov, V. (1998). *Stanislavski in Rehearsal* (C. Edwards, Trans). Routledge.

CHAPTER 3

Second Phase: 1903–08, Placing Improvisation in the Production Process

Abstract By the end of the first decade of work at the Moscow Art Theatre, Stanislavsky's reputation as a highly creative director and creator of dazzling production plans was cemented forever. However, the emphasis on production plans far from tells the whole story of Stanislavsky's methods between 1903 and 1908. In other words, he still found space for the application of improvisation. In these years Stanislavsky used improvisation in the following three ways: (i) to call on the assistance of the actors when creating abstract, non-realistic mises-en-scène, synonymous with the symbolist plays that were popular at the time; (ii) in rehearsal, when he himself offered improvised demonstrations in order to get his meaning across to the actors; (iii) as a technique for actors to explore their characters, which included improvising in everyday life.

Keywords Mise-en-scène · Symbolism · Demonstration · Rehearsal · Characterisation · Everyday life

A stern reprimand from his father over the company he was keeping led Stanislavsky to form the Society of Arts and Literature in 1888 as an amateur theatre group which, however, took matters of repertoire and production very seriously. It was at the Society of Arts and Literature that

Stanislavsky started to make a name for himself as an actor, even if these years (1888–98) and, subsequently, the first few years of the Moscow Art Theatre (between 1898 and 1903), also evidenced a Stanislavsky at his most directorial. Initially he was not especially attracted to directing, given that he always favoured acting. He took on his first directing duties when no other director came forward from among his colleagues, and quickly found himself to be very inventive when creating stage material. Bella Merlin (2003: 9–12) describes Stanislavsky's then approach to production as that of a director-dictator, which comes as no surprise given the influence which the Meinengen company and its director Ludwig Chronegk exerted on him (Stanislavski, 2008: 113–16). Stanislavsky's work method relied heavily on the creation of a mise-en-scène, or a production plan that featured 'all of the resources of stage performance: décor, lighting, music and acting' as well as 'the activity that consists in arranging, in a particular time and space' these same resources (Veinstein in Pavis, 1998: 363). In his role as a director Stanislavsky brought these two definitions together by creating a performance score comprising of a vast amount of detail emanating from his creative imagination: how actors spoke, moved, behaved on stage, the costumes worn, light, sound effects, and music used, scenery, set design, props, etc. were all details that Stanislavsky conceived alone in his study. This production plan was then arranged, or translated, into stage action during the rehearsals, with the actors and other theatre artists (composers, designers, prop-makers, etc.) expected to bring the director's plan to life. While not completely eliminated, the creative input of the actor was severely restricted. In this way of working, the director also becomes the orchestrator tasked with bringing the whole together into an organic piece of theatre.

With the exception of the occasional indulgence, Stanislavsky's barrage of production details was not an end in itself. It rather created the mood and atmosphere of the performance in which the spectators immersed themselves. The realistic details of Stanislavsky's production plans were also intended to help the actors shed false theatrical convention and engage emotionally with the character. For example, when working on *The Cherry Orchard* (1903), Stanislavsky 'needed atmospheric devices to get his actors off the ground' (Benedetti, 1999: 141), even if Chekhov often found these devices unnecessary.[1] Productions like the Society's *Uriel Acosta* (1895), *The Assumption of Hannele* (1896), and *Othello* (1896) made a name for their spectacular reproduction of locale, while others from the first years of the MAT—like *The Seagull* (1898) and *An*

Enemy of the People (1900)—impressed by their acting. Ever the experimenter, and successful though these productions undoubtedly were, Stanislavsky was however reluctant to stay too much in one artistic place. He always understood that repetition leads to stagnation. Therefore, while a number of subsequent productions which I will discuss in this section—e.g. *Ghosts* (1905), *Children of the Sun* (1905), *Woe from Wit* (1906), *The Drama of Life* (1907), *The Life of Man* (1907), and *The Blue Bird* (1908)—were still characterised by a production-plan approach to staging, they envisage a Stanislavsky who was starting to pursue significant (if not always successful) experiments in the inner technique of the actor. The following quotations sheds light on the challenges of the time and the relevant conclusions Stanislavsky derived:

> Without realising it, [in *The Drama of Life*] I had hidden behind my collaborators, i.e. the directors, the designers, the costume department, the composers, etc., profiting from the fact that in a combined effort the audience cannot distinguish the work of one department from the other. [...] How many practical examples could we quote of productions in which the actors hide behind the director, the designer, and the composer? How often the background obscures the very essence of our art—acting. (Stanislavski, 2008: 264–265)
> [In *The Life of Man*,] [w]e were able to achieve [a range of] external effects thanks to black velvet, which played an important role in the production. The play and the production had a great success. [...] Despite the show's great success, I was unhappy with the results, as I understood perfectly well that it had brought nothing new to our art. (Stanislavski, 2008: 276)

While Stanislavsky was disappointed that these experiments did not yield the hoped-for results in advancing the art of the actor, a sensitive observer like Alisa Koonen still underlined his skill as a director and orchestrator of effects. His crowd scenes in *Woe from Wit*, for example, achieved 'a perfect sense of style [through which] [...] the Griboedov era itself lived and sounded' (in Vinogradskaia Vol. 2 2003: 34). In any case, the emphasis on production plans far from tells the whole story of Stanislavsky's methods of the time. In other words, he still found space for the application of improvisation. In these years Stanislavsky used improvisation in the following three ways:

(i) to call on the assistance of the actors when creating abstract, non-realistic mises-en-scène, synonymous with the symbolist plays that were popular at the time;
(ii) in rehearsal, when he himself offered improvised demonstrations in order to get his meaning across to the actors;
(iii) as a technique for actors to explore their characters; this again included improvising in everyday life.

Several plays that Stanislavsky staged between 1903–08 were out of his comfort zone. He had excelled in Realism and Naturalism but, inspired by the more abstract art that was surrounding him, he tried his hand at depicting the unreal and the spiritual on stage. Maurice Maeterlinck provided a key reference point, with Stanislavsky bookending this attempt at the intangible by staging a bill of three shorts plays by the Belgian playwright (1904) and the aforementioned *The Blue Bird* four years later. (Knut Hamsun's *The Drama of Life* and Leonid Andreev's *The Life of Man* were other productions in a similar vein.) New plays demanded alternative forms, and improvisation became a means to discover these forms and to populate the mise-en-scène. For *The Blue Bird*, for instance, Benedetti says that Stanislavsky wanted new childlike designs, new sets, and new music instead of typical orchestrations. This was possible only after 'several months of work and experiments [...] [that] included exercises and improvisations for the actors and the extras' (Benedetti, 1999: 179). The more collaborative nature of improvisation was particularly important given the new ground that Stanislavsky was treading on here; the play featured roles such as Fire, Light, Water, Stars, and so on, and required animal behaviours and traits for others like Cat, Cow, Wolf, and Rabbit. Vladimir Nemirovich-Danchenko, the co-founder with Stanislavsky of the MAT, confirmed the use of these improvisations in a letter to his wife: '[Stanislavsky] asked the actors to portray a cat, a dog, a rooster, and so on. This whole crowd meowed, barked, squeaked, screamed—and he was delighted. You see, he needs this for *The Blue Bird*' (Vinogradskaia Vol. 2 2003: 79). Rehearsals for *The Life of Man* included physical improvisations with actors crawling on the floor (80).

Stanislavsky's then use of improvisation was embroiled in a broader power struggle within the MAT. It was his own practical way through which to criticise the overall work of the Art Theatre which, spearheaded by Nemirovich-Danchenko, he felt was becoming too 'literal' (Benedetti, 1999: 153). In a meeting held in May 1905 to discuss

The Drama of Life, Stanislavsky boldly asserted that his work on the production was to start from improvisation. This statement shocked Nemirovich-Danchenko, who as a theatre-maker always gave precedence to the text and to the intentions of the author.[2] What would have bothered Nemirovich-Danchenko even more was that Vsevolod Meyerhold, who at the time was engaged by Stanislavsky as the artistic director of the Theatre-Studio, was also present at the meeting. Nemirovich-Danchenko was always concerned when someone got too close to Stanislavsky, and in this meeting he saw such influence taking place in front of his eyes and, to make matters worse, with a persona non grata like Meyerhold! Irina Vinogradskaia describes the meeting as follows:

> After the reading, V. E. Meyerhold and Stanislavsky propose a new way of rehearsing, without preliminary discussions and analysis of the play at the table, without drawing up a director's plan—a method in which the actors themselves 'with their own improvisations' suggest the features of the character and of the mises-en-scène. (Vinogradskaia Vol. 1 2003: 496)

Nemirovich-Danchenko reacted strongly. He argued that such a method was not only a waste of time but that it would also ruin the play. He made his feelings clear to Stanislavsky in a letter dated 8–10 June 1905: 'You wanted the actors to go on stage and play excerpts from the play when neither they nor the director had any character image!' (496).

For all his bravado, Stanislavsky started drafting the production plan of *The Drama of Life* soon after, in July in fact (in Vinogradskaia Vol. 1 2003: 512). This makes me think that more than a real intention to initiate the work on the production via improvisation, Stanislavsky's statement was a ploy to flare up Nemirovich-Danchenko. This is especially the case considering that the two had been at loggerheads for quite some time, with tensions mounting as a result of Nemirovich-Danchenko's treatment of Savva Morozov, Maxim Gorky, and Leopold Sulerzhitsky (again among Stanislavsky's closest collaborators at the time), disagreements on the staging of *Ghosts*, conflict over the meaning of their respective veto,[3] and Nemirovich-Danchenko's overall attempt to gain control of the theatre's management[4]—there really was never a dull moment at the MAT! In the end, rehearsals for *The Drama of Life* continued well into 1905 and 1906, with the play finally opening on the 8 February 1907.

One consequence of creating a production plan was that Stanislavsky found himself soaking in the atmosphere that he was creating. This provided him with a knowledge of all the roles, of their actions and intentions since, to all intents, he was the one who was formulating them. Such a deep knowledge of the roles helped Stanislavsky to improvise on the spot during rehearsals and to demonstrate what he had in mind or was looking for from the actors. Even Nemirovich-Danchenko noted that Stanislavsky was particularly inspiring when he put rational explanations to the side in order to improvise and to directly demonstrate his meaning to the actors: 'When you are enthralled by the depth of the stage image, and you show actors on stage how to express this or that—for example, to Kachalov in *Ghosts* and thousands of other similar cases—then you are a great director' (Vinogradskaia Vol. 1 2003: 484). Stanislavsky proved to be a master of such improvised demonstrations:

> He corrects someone, takes a pose, shows how to stand up and sit down. If the public, the spectators [...] had the opportunity to attend his rehearsals, to see what this magician is doing, how, while remaining himself, he immediately transforms into many characters, deepening them and their relationships in every moment, lighting up, flaring up, becoming young and old, experiencing the lives of many people—then they would experience more excitement than from the performances themselves. (Ulyanov in Vinogradskaia Vol. 2 2003: 51)

More than prepared pieces intended for showing, these demonstrations were spontaneously dictated by the uniqueness of a rehearsal moment and the difficulties which an actor was encountering. They were improvisations that lived in the present moment and to which they answered directly, with a concern for the present moment fast becoming a key denominator to his changing approach to improvisation (see especially Fourth Phase below). Benedetti, for example, remarks that one such demonstration given to Olga Knipper when rehearsing *Ghosts* 'was the *spontaneous* reaction of an experienced professional, which he was not able yet to analyse' (Benedetti, 1999: 154; emphasis added).[5]

Stanislavsky's improvised demonstrations were directed towards individual actors and corresponded to a specific stage task. In the example above he assisted Knipper; in another rehearsal for *Ghosts* he assisted the actress Margarita Savitskaya by demonstrating her character's way of walking (Stanislavskii, 1993b: 251). His improvisations however impacted the other actors on the stage. Koonen recounts one such episode. The company was rehearsing Gorky's *Children of the Sun*, when Olga Melania, one of the actresses, was finding it difficult to throw herself greedily at Vasily Kacholov's feet, who was playing Protasov. Stanislavsky again improvised in front of her, and while this demonstration was seemingly intended to help Melania, it also brought the best out of Kachalov: 'Falling to his knees in front of Kachalov, he [Stanislavsky] hugged him so tightly that Vasily Ivanovich [Kachalov] could barely stay on his feet and began to fight off the hugs with real Protasov-like despair' (Koonen, 1985: 27). Koonen offers another example from the same rehearsals. The actress N. N. Litovtseva, playing the maid Fima, could not execute a particular run across the stage. Stanislavsky first explained the depth of such a seemingly small stage action. He remained unsatisfied with her performance, until 'in the end he got up on the stage and in a very funny way began to show the vulgar movements of Fima's hips and the defiant tapping of her heels' (27).

Given the image we often take for granted of Stanislavsky, that of a formidable teacher who time and time again extrapolated creative performances from his actors, such instances of work where he is demonstrating to the actors what they should do seem to be a step backwards in his development as a theatre maker. Stanislavsky certainly used improvisation to demonstrate the outer characteristics, results even, of a role (e.g. showing Savitskaya how her character should walk), but this outer work should not be dismissed. The discovery of such outer characteristics is an essential part of creating a role, as Stanislavsky was to recognise again when he erroneously side-lined outer work from *The Drama of Life* to focus on inner life instead (Stanislavski, 2008: 271–72). While it is all well and good to see Stanislavsky as an indefatigable experimenter who was never quite satisfied with his results, it is also worth remembering that he was also a director working with actors and experiencing the typical challenges of the profession: difficulty to get across to the actors, increasing production pressures, unexpected circumstances, and so on. Improvised demonstrations assisted Stanislavsky in navigating these challenges, including helping actors overcome some stumbling block and to move forward with the production process.

Another use of improvisation cut deeper than straightforward demonstrations. Improvisation was also used to explore nuanced characterisation. Evidence of this use is found in Stanislavsky's letters to Vera Kotliarevskaia, an actress of the Alexandrinsky Theatre. She had expressed admiration of Stanislavsky's performance as Trigorin in *The Seagull*, after which he quickly brought her into his confidence. In fact, Stanislavsky often shared with her several significant matters, including his worry on *The Cherry Orchard*, even remarking that Chekhov's presence at rehearsals was confusing the actors (Vinogradskaia Vol. 1 2003: 449); the poor financial state of the MAT (Stanislavskii, 1960: 329–30); and his frustrations with Moscow's artistic circles and critics (221). Other passages in these letters contain typical details and anecdotes told between actors. Thus Stanislavsky spoke a number of times of being over worked or ill, about the difficulties with some role (including Brutus), the relationship with his wife, and the general state in Russia. These instances offer a glimpse into Stanislavsky's private world as he tried to come to terms with a life in the theatre. However, references to acting and to the System are also evident. Kotliarevskaia received early drafts of the Handbook for the Dramatic Artist that Stanislavsky was working on and, in a letter dated 1 July 1905, he conveyed how eagerly he was waiting for her feedback, underlining further his respect towards her as an artist and friend: 'You are silent about my notes. [...] I need your criticism, not praise' (Vinogradskaia Vol. 1 2003: 507). She also joined Stanislavsky and his family during the milestone Finnish holiday of 1906 where the System was first conceived. Here, he read her further drafts of his manual (Vinogradskaia Vol. 2 2003: 33).

Perhaps it was because he could not work directly with Kotliarevskaia that Stanislavsky suggested an improvisation-heavy approach to working on a role, an approach which she could carry out on her own. The discovery of a character's way of walking, their gait, was a problem experienced by the actress. To solve this, Stanislavsky encouraged her to practice in everyday life: 'Walk with your legs twisted, with the hunched gait of a decrepit old woman, the regal gait of a queen [...]. Let your feet touch real earth: raw, wet, alive' (Stanislavskii, 1960: 210–11). Such improvisations in the everyday life of the actress (more on this below) were particularly helpful to break the bonds of convention. A more detailed letter dated 1 July 1905 is quoted at length by Jean Benedetti. To work on Charlotta in *The Cherry Orchard*, Stanislavsky asked Kotliarevskaia to 'shut yourself up and play whatever goes through your head'; possible scenarios included a reaction to a marriage proposal, finding alternative employment at a circus or café, and singing songs which Charlotta would like. Benedetti evaluates Stanislavsky's advice as follows: 'This contains in embryo much that was to be developed later: the exploration of character through improvisation, setting the character in new imaginary circumstances, not foreseen by the author, as a means of stimulating the actor's imagination' (Benedetti, 1999: 168).

In 1905, such an exploration of the character through improvisation seems to have already become a key method for Stanislavsky. He underlined further this approach in an interview published that year in the newspaper *Russian Theatre*:

> We do not touch the play. We take a type and improvise all the various situations in which he may find himself. Take the footman Peter, for example, in *Ivanov*—he only has to stand in the study and listen to the conversation of the gentlemen. Meanwhile, the actor who played him—Mr Leontiev—imagined what Peter was like in the kitchen, and what he was like with his wife; so Peter's appearance on stage is *only a random episode from his life that is happening behind the scenes*. Or Ivanov...First, imagine what he is like with the peasants, what he is like in various situations, what his opinions are of the district authorities, about populism; try to understand what it means to live like Ivanov, to think like Ivanov, and to walk down the street like Ivanov, and *then, once you understand all this, take what Chekhov wrote in the play as a distinct part in Ivanov's life which you can now act out*. Then the vitality of your image will increase a lot, the audience (and you yourself) will not feel that you are an artist who began to act only when he appeared in front of the footlights. No, in front them the audience will see a living person who before entering the stage has lived his life. (Stanislavskii, 1994: 445; emphasis in original)

What Stanislavsky valued in this exercise is that it gives birth to a range of unexpected details, rendered all the more simply and naturally because they are lived through in an improvisation rather than thought out rationally. In such an approach there is Stanislavsky's own way of highlighting body-based research processes in the character, a continuation of his readings of the professional actors discussed in the First Phase but also a precursor of his later work on physical action.

Improvisations on imaginary circumstances is a technique that Stanislavsky steadily used from now on, even if such an approach would be pushed to the side by the more text-focused études of Active Analysis.[6] In any case, it is to be noted that during the first decade of the 1900's Stanislavsky was asking actors to carry out preparatory improvisations at home as a way of giving them more responsibility. In November 1903, for example, while Stanislavsky was at the theatre rehearsing the production plan of *The Cherry Orchard*, Knipper was improvising at home images for the role of Ranevskaya. She put on a range of elegant dresses in order to approximate the feeling of a chic woman (Vinogradskaia Vol. 1 2003: 436). It was no longer enough for the actors to simply turn up to the rehearsals and passively assimilate the director's production plan.[7] They were expected to contribute, to work privately on their roles, and to come to rehearsals prepared; invariably, Stanislavsky could feel when this preparatory work was not carried out (Vinogradskaia Vol. 2 2003: 113).

More evidence of the use of improvisation to explore character can be found in the director's diary that Stanislavsky kept when working on the play *Ivan Mironich* (1904–5).[8] This is a play, written by E. Chirikov, which Stanislavsky initially liked, even if his enthusiasm for the play would later cool down.[9] Any analysis of this play and its rehearsal process is a valuable addition to our knowledge of Stanislavsky, given that the production does not feature in any discussion about his work.[10] Ostensibly, the direction of the production was credited to Vasily Luzhsky, even if Stanislavsky's contribution to the production was significant—a note in the first edition of the Collected Works says that 'Stanislavsky, as the main director of the Theatre, made significant adjustments to Luzhsky's work, correcting and reworking a lot of it. He was actually the artistic director of the production' (Stanislavskii, 1958: 587). Chirikov also noted Stanislavsky's involvement, saying that he 'appears [at rehearsal] and suddenly breaks everything and begins to rebuild' (Vinogradskaia Vol. 1 2003: 471).

Stanislavsky's notes for *Ivan Mironich* are substantial, totalling some 47 pages and reproduced in both editions of his Collected Works. In these notes Stanislavsky 'tried to formulate his requirements for the actor's technique. He is thinking about the ways of creating a close-up on the inner world of a person' (Vinogradskaia Vol. 1 2003: 470). Improvisation again played a significant role. In an entry dated 14 January 1905, when Act 3 was being rehearsed, Stanislavsky reflected on the director's contribution to the actor's work on a role. He identified six points. The first two suggest table work. The director first explains what he wants to achieve with the production as a whole, after which an analysis is made not of the characters per se but of what the other characters say on a particular role. The third point relays how the director evokes memories in the actor, making them recall past instances from their lives but as needed by the plot and the character. Improvisation appears in the fourth point as a way of embodying these memories:

If an actor is talented, sensitive and observant, my God, what memories he will bring in, what types or hints of the human types he will show! 'I knew the person who was talking "this way"', and in an improvised, invented scene he will draw an image, then another, he will give the director an idea. [...] Each of the actors will vie to find and show the desired character. Then the director will only have to notice and feel what the actor has for this role, and give him some suggestions of his own. [...] During such rehearsals, one could mistake the theatre for a madhouse, and the actors for clowns. Everyone is rushing around and speaking in different voices, as the artist's first strokes are rough, exaggerated, and unfinished. From them, however, one can deduce the future character. (Stanislavskii, 1958: 234)

A significant implication of this approach is that improvisation becomes a kind of channel between the actor and the director, or an opportunity for them to collaborate together. The actor is tasked with bringing the raw material to rehearsal, which the director subsequently polishes and renders into theatrically strong images. As mentioned above, Stanislavsky came to see *Ivan Mironich* as a weak play that needed a lot of added flair and imagination. This extra flair was previously provided by the director, through the use of a dazzling mise-en-scène, but here Stanislavsky shifted at least part of this responsibility onto the actor and the depths that he discovers, or even invents, in the character. The compositional hand of the director reappears in point 5, where they endeavour to place the improvisations of the actors in the framework of the play. A more collaborative atmosphere between the actors and the director is thus created, nourishing in turn a less hierarchical atmosphere in the rehearsal room. Both parties contribute in their own unique ways to the production process, something which Stanislavsky would develop further at the First Studio by also including the playwright in the mix (see Third Phase below). Apart from the new inroads that improvisation suggested when creating stage work, it was in the way that it undergirds a collaborative attitude in the theatre process that was to have long-term repercussions on Stanislavsky's development as a theatre maker. Finally, point 6 is more overarching in nature. It speaks of the awareness which actors develop when they understand and feel what in an improvisation is typical of their character and what is superfluous.

The use of improvisation to explore characterisation was also one of the conclusions that Stanislavsky derived from the 1907–08 season. Improvisations are here more forcefully located to the everyday life of the actors.

In a first instance, they help the actor explore a character's mannerisms; note another reference to the manner of one's walking (the gait) in the following quotation:

> If the play made an impression on the artist and he felt kindred feelings, he will begin to itch creatively.
> [...] So, for example, going up to his apartment on the top floor, he will no longer simply walk with his own gait. He will try to capture someone's else gait, the one of a decrepit old man maybe, a drunken cadet, or some fat priest. (Stanislavskii, 1993b: 299)

The discovery of these manners is the first step towards creating a role. More elaborated improvisations in everyday life are attempted, similar to those at the Alekseev Circle discussed in the First Phase, with the crucial difference that now improvisations evidence both a physical or action-based level as well as a deeper, more psychological attempt at understanding the depths of a role. Take, for instance, an actor working on the role of a sick, old man:

> The actor imagines that he is a decrepit, sick, old man. He hasn't left the apartment for a month, but today, on the 20th of the month, he had to leave. He returns home with his pension, but he constantly feels that he might have dropped the money. He constantly checks his pocket and searches all over himself; genuinely frightened, he instinctively begins to look around him for the missing money, but then his trembling hand accidentally touches the greasy piece of paper, and the old man's face calms down. [...] Standing still [...] the old man complains that, notwithstanding his long service, he is forced to experience such torment. They could have brought his pension home; they could have, he deserved it, he deserved it. He served with faith, truth, and righteousness. He served the Tsar, God, and the Fatherland. (Stanislavskii, 1993b: 299)

Stanislavsky adds that this might be a 'primitive image' or draft, and that discoveries found in such improvisations can also quickly turn into an empty shell devoid of intention. This is especially the case once the improvisation is repeated. Their potential is in that they help the actor to move towards more creative work, serving as an important first step in the creative process. They also give actors experience of improvising when something unexpected, such as a mistake, happens in performance, an ability which Stanislavsky elsewhere related to the actor's resourcefulness.[11] For example, how does the improvisation on the stairs change if a neighbour comes out of her apartment? In such cases the actor improvises accordingly while remaining in character: 'He tripped [...,] cursed and immediately embarrassed himself, as a lady who probably saw everything was silently coming out of the door. To smooth out the awkwardness, the actor acted as if he had actually tripped and was now dusting off his trousers' (300).

During these years Stanislavsky also started giving more thought to the training of his actors. Lessons carried out at his home became more common. These lessons are described briefly by Alisa Koonen. By her second year at the Art Theatre (she joined around 1905) Koonen had already fallen under Stanislavsky's rather than Nemirovich-Danchenko's radar, who had his own group of 'students'. Koonen says that 'most classes [with Stanislavsky] were improvisations' in which something unexpected was always offered. In one of these he asked her to dance a waltz with a chair instead of a real partner, or to play a person she had met and whom she found memorable: 'Once I portrayed a friend of my grandmother, a fat, young German woman, the owner of the May Dew beauty salon. I improvised her conversation on the phone with a client' (Koonen 1985: 40). Evident here, I feel, is an attempt to use improvisation as a way of developing the actor's technical skill—the improvisation with the chair, for example, allows the participant to work on imaginary circumstances, posture, and focus; the improvised conversation on the phone necessitates an understanding of timing and logic. It was to be a durable application of improvisation, one that would feature prominently in the next phase of work synonymous with the First Studio.

Exploring character through improvisation
- This exercise is to be treated from the point of view of the director working with a group of actors. Choose a short scene from a play—Chekhov's would lend themselves well to this exercise—and create a detailed production plan. Bella Merlin (2003) adapts several moments from Stanislavsky's production plan to *The Seagull*, which can be used as an example. Transmit this production plan to the actors, and try to be as precise as possible in terms of locale, mood, rhythms, props and their handling, and, most importantly, the actors' acting, their voices, movements, actions, behaviours, groupings, and

interpretations. Ask actors about their reactions to this exercise. How did they feel? Did they find the process at all helpful? Was it restrictive? In what sense? Finally, direct them to this question: how do you find creative freedom in the production plan?
- Remove a clear and tangible acting element from the production plan, such as a contained and discernible series of actions with an object. Encourage actors to improvise an alternative, and to experiment in incorporating this in the broader mise-en-scène. Ask actors again for their feedback, about what worked but also the difficulties they encountered.
- The following exercise is an adaptation of Jacques Copeau's animal study as recounted in Evans (2009: 129–35). In Copeau's vision this work is not an end in itself, in the sense that the aim is not to reproduce the animal behaviour. It rather serves as a way 'of learning about character through imaginative exploration of mind and body, based on a strong external stimulus' (130). In a nutshell, the process of animal study involves (i) the observation of a particular animal (ii) elucidation of its main traits (environment, movement qualities, relationship between different body parts, breadth, intentions, and so on) (iii) improvisation on these traits, starting from a sleeping position and then transitioning into walking and further, emotionally-informed, movement. As a development to this exercise, whittle down the improvisation to a repeatable score, one that might be inserted in a production plan to a fantastical play like *The Blue Bird*. This is the process which Stanislavsky would have followed while producing the play. What criteria do you apply to choose some moments of the improvisations over others?
- Experiment with the traits or qualities of a character you are rehearsing by carrying out improvisations in your own everyday life. Initially consider the ways in which the character carries themselves, uses objects, walks, sits down, and so on. Compare these physical traits with your own natural way of carrying yourself. Discuss differences with people who are close to you. Extend the improvisations by going to places which might interest the character, all the time reacting to the surroundings from their (rather than your) particular point of view. Is this character-building exercise helpful, especially when today many advise about the importance of separating work from private life?
- At the studio or rehearsal room, improvise scenes from the character's life which are not in the author's text. Stanislavsky's advice

to Kotliarevskaia when she was working on Charlotta in *The Cherry Orchard* is an example. However, rather than simply going through the motions of doing an improvisation, consider what you will take from each improvisation and how this connects with your overarching interpretation of the character and its performance. What is the improvisation helping you to concretely discover about the character? Extend this exercise by carrying out improvisations between two or more characters.

Notes

1. On Chekhov's objections to Stanislavsky's production methods see Shevtsova (2020: 196–97). Stanislavsky felt justified in using these atmospheric devices because of the inexperienced actors that he was working with up to the first years of the MAT (Stanislavski, 2008: 196–97).
2. Nemirovich was already far from happy when two months before Stanislavsky wanted to change some lines in Ibsen's *Ghosts* to accommodate the actor's physical work (the carpenter working on a door). Stanislavsky remarked that this particular physical addition made 'everything come alive. Only to do this we shall have to change the author's opening words and move sentences around. What else can we do? It seems to me not to do it is just pedantry' (in Benedetti, 1999: 153).
3. On how Stanislavsky and Nemirovich-Danchenko's veto system at the MAT—'The literary veto goes to Nemirovich-Danchenko, the artistic to Stanislavski'—quickly created problems between the two see Aquilina (2020: 41–42).
4. For a detailed reconstruction of the tension between Stanislavsky and Nemirovich-Danchenko during these years see Benedetti (1999: 150–83). Key letters of the period can be found in Benedetti (1991: 193–236).
5. Stanislavsky's improvisation involved taking on 'the insolent coquettishness, the lust of life and the predatory essence of Regina's character [the role Knipper was playing]' by focusing on his eye work, a hunched physicality, and corresponding hand gestures (Verigina in Benedetti 1999: 153).

6. In Active Analysis, Stanislavsky's final, more holistic approach to creating a role, the emphasis is placed on improvising on concrete given circumstances as encoded in a text, rather than inventing new imaginary scenarios. In this way, improvisations become an étude, i.e. a study, of the text and its given circumstances. On the difference between improvisation and étude see Carnicke (2019).
7. This is what Stanislavsky had to say after the first reading of *The Blue Bird* on the need for the actors to work on their own at home and to come prepared to rehearsals: 'We will put a lot of work together, a lot of attention and love into studying the play, but this is not enough…It is necessary that, in addition to this common work, you prepare yourself on your own. I'm talking about your observations in your own personal life which will expand your imagination and sensitivity. Make friends with children, delve into their world, take a closer look at nature and the things that surround us, make friends with a dog and a cat and look through their eyes into their souls more often. You will do what Maeterlinck did before writing the play, and this path will bring you closer to the author.' (Stanislavskii, 1993a: 121–122).
8. *Ivan Mironich* opened on the 28 January 1905.
9. In his memoirs Chirikov remarked that at the play's reading (7 May 1904) Stanislavsky had laughed 'like a high school student' (in Vinogradskaia, 2003 vol. 1: 455); soon afterwards Stanislavsky however remarked that this was a weak play which the actors and directors have to 'complete' by working together (476).
10. As far as I could ascertain, the production of *Ivan Mironich* does not feature in sources by Benedetti (1999), Shevtsova (2020), or Carnicke (2009). Senelick mentions it only in passing, either in a broader discussion about the repertoire, or to remark that it was sub-standard play (Senelick, 2013: 192 and 196).
11. 'When a chair accidentally falls on stage, something is dropped, or furniture is placed in the wrong place, it is necessary that the first person to notice it plays on this accident and puts the thing in its place. If he is confused by this surprising occurrence or diligently bypasses it (which he would not do in life), this would show the cowardice of the actor and makes the audience forget about reality and feel sorry and amused by the actor's lack of resourcefulness.' (Stanislavskii, 1993b: 261).

REFERENCES

Aquilina, S. (2020). *Modern theatre in Russia: Tradition building and transmission processes*. Bloomsbury.
Benedetti, J. (Ed. and Trans.) (1991). *The Moscow art theatre letters*. Methuen.
Benedetti, J. (1999). *Stanislavski: His life and art*. Methuen.
Carnicke, S. (2009). *Stanislavsky in focus* (2nd ed.). Routledge.
Carnicke, S. (2019). Improvisations and etudes: An experiment in Active Analysis. *Stanislavski Studies*, 7(1), 17–35.
Evans, M. (Ed.). (2015). *The actor training reader*. Routledge.
Koonen A. G. (1985). *Stranicii zhizni* [Pages of a life], ed. by Y. Rybakova (2nd ed.). Iskusstvo.
Merlin, B. (2003). *Konstantin Stanislavsky*. Routledge.
Pavis, P. (1998) *Dictionary of theatre. Terms, concepts, and analysis* (C. Shantz, Trans.). University of Toronto Press.
Senelick, L. (ed. and trans.) (2013). *Stanislavsky: His life in letters*.
Shevtsova, M. (2020). *Rediscovering Stanislavsky*. Cambridge University Press.
Stanislavski, K. (2008) *My life in art* (J. Benedetti, Trans.). Routledge.
Stanislavskii, K. (1958) *Sobranie Sochinenii Tom 5* [Collected Works in 8 Volumes, Volume 5]. Iskusstvo.
Stanislavskii, K. (1960). *Sobranie Sochinenii Tom 7* [Collected Works in 8 Volumes, Volume 7]. Iskusstvo.
Stanislavskii, K. (1993a). *Sobranie Sochinenii Tom 5.1* [Collected Works in 9 volumes, Volume 5.1]. Iskusstvo.
Stanislavskii, K. (1993b). *Sobranie Sochinenii Tom 5.2* [Collected Works in 9 volumes, Volume 5.2]. Iskusstvo.
Stanislavskii, K. (1994). *Sobranie Sochinenii Tom 6* [Collected Works in 9 volumes, Volume 6]. Iskusstvo
Vinogradskaia, I. N. (2003). *Zhizn i tvorchestvo K. S. Stanislavskogo*. [The life and work of K. S. Stanislavsky, 4 volumes]. Moscow Art Theatre Press.

CHAPTER 4

Third Phase: 1912–16, The First Studio and Stanislavsky's Offshoots

Abstract The First Studio opened in 1912 as a space where Stanislavsky could experiment with his System. This chapter reappraises the first few years of the Studio (until Suler's death in 1916) from the point of view of improvisation. As can be expected from a versatile theatre-maker like Stanislavsky, improvisation at the First Studio saw several uses. Scenarios were improvised on, not as an end in itself, but to work on a technical element of the System such as concentration, communication with a partner, rhythm, emotional recall, etc. Improvisation also took the form of Gorky's Method, an experiment which Stanislavsky conducted where the actor-students, in collaboration with a playwright and a director/leader, improvise on set scenarios to create new plays. Stanislavsky did not steer singlehandedly the work of the Studio. Much fell on Leopold Sulerzhitsky, the Studio's leader, and on participants like Yevgeny Vakhtangov, Michael Chekhov, and Valentin Smyshlaev. Stanislavsky's offshoots give improvisation a decidedly contemporary edge, either by resolving the structure-improvisation conundrum, or by linking improvisation with what today we would refer to as 'devised performance'.

Keywords Gorky's Method · Yevgeny Vakhtangov · Michael Chekhov · Leopold Sulerzhitsky · Valentin Smyshlaev · Improvisation

The Blue Bird was, essentially, a director's play, the logical conclusion to Stanislavsky's directorial phase. As Benedetti (1999: 184) writes, it 'was his last "spectacular" as a director and a fitting culmination to a brilliant series of productions. That phase was now behind him'. Building on the experiments of the Second Phase, Stanislavsky's focus now turned with ever increasing energy on the work of the actor. Initially, this involved rehearsing a play according to the embryonic System. Terms such as 'nail' (the precursor of the throughaction) and 'circle' (later developed in the circles of concentration) started to make an appearance in rehearsals (185), as did the fragmentation of a text in bits and the search for psychological states, emotions, and feelings. While initial positive results in productions like *The Inspector General* (1908) and *A Month in the Country* (1909) were noted, the doubt expressed by several actors of the old guard, especially Knipper and even his wife Lilina, prompted Stanislavsky to look elsewhere for a space that was more conducive to the research that he had in mind. The modus operandi of the main Theatre, with its budgets, deadlines, ingrained practices, but also struggles for power and authority, proved antithetical to Stanislavsky's experimental zeal.

The formation of a studio provided Stanislavsky with a solution. Bringing together a group of promising youngsters that included Yevgeny Vakhtangov, Michael Chekhov, Richard Boleslavsky, Serafima Birman, Maria Ouspenskaya, and others, and placed under the direction of Leopold Sulerzhitsky (Suler), the First Studio was founded in September 1912 as a space for research, experimentation, and pedagogical work[1]; in fact, it was at the Studio that the understanding of 'pedagogy' as a combination of teaching (transmission of technique) and research (finding new solutions to stage problems) was first crystallised.[2] The choice to work with beginning actors who had some acting knowledge was both an inspired and a necessary one.[3] Young actors already had some experience of the difficulties posed by the acting profession, but they were still unfixed in their ways and therefore more open to new and possibly radical approaches.

The First Studio was conceived as a laboratory. This means that the majority of the work was channelled through trial and error, technical exercises, short sketches and, at most, scenes or extracts from plays rather than the staging of full performances. Consequently, the Studio afforded its participants that biggest luxury in theatre, namely the time to work without the pressure of opening night. The students quickly formed a close-knit community. In practical terms, the communal aspect of the Studio translated into a collective approach towards research. Any participant could initiate an aspect of work, propose an exercise, or set forth an investigation, which the other members were expected to fully support (Leach, 2003: 79 and Gordon, 1987: 43). Vakhtangov even wrote that everyone was a leader (Malaev-Babel, 2012: 57). Studio participants also shared a fervent belief in the System, seeing it as both a way out of theatre automatisms as well as a foothold towards a stable place in theatre; in a letter dated 25 September 1912 to his daughter Kira, Stanislavsky remarked that the Studio had indeed achieved 'a common denominator' which everyone follows (in Senelick, 2013: 331). The difficult work conditions which they shared—sessions were often held at night—helped them to gravitate further towards one another. More pleasantly, they also lived together during the summer months on a piece of land which Stanislavsky purchased for the Studio at Evpatoria and where they built their own houses and shared daily chores (Stanislavski, 2008a: 311). These circumstances imbued participants with the deepest commitment to ethics and aesthetics, with the whole venture becoming an idealistic dream to create a new 'spiritual order of actors' (Gauss, 1999: 37). It has to be said, however, that this dream soon gave way to the disorders that are synonymous with theatre (Shevtsova, 2020: 145–46). The members of the First Studio were, after all, human beings prone to laxity, desire for public gratification, bickering over parts, and so on. They were especially keen to use the Studio to get the roles which were unavailable to them at the main house (Malaev-Babel, 2012: 67). Still, in September 1912 the possibility of a Studio that would serve as a bastion for truth instead of lies, in theatre and in life, seemed like a concrete possibility.[4]

Before tackling improvisation at the Studio, a brief mention of a couple of points is necessary. First, the First Studio is where the reality of Stanislavsky's offshoots, figures like the aforementioned Suler, Vakhtangov, and Chekhov, needs to be given attention. These were far from passive participants. They each exhibited strong personalities who interpreted Stanislavsky's System in important and thoroughly unique ways; Chekhov would even say that such interpretations are a given since 'it is inevitable that each of us who worked with Stanislavsky would understand and interpret the System in his own way and according to his own particular individuality' (in Mollica, 1989: 76). Amongst them I also include the often-maligned Valentin Smyshlaev, who was reproved by Stanislavsky for incorrectly understanding and even appropriating some elements of the System as his own. To my eyes, however, Smyshlaev offers an interesting case of performance hybridity, when he brought together production processes based on the System (particularly text analysis) with collective creation as theorised on by Platon Kerzhentsev (Aquilina, 2020: 74–80). Suler, Vakhtangov, Chekhov, and Smyshlaev were very different theatre-makers who shared a keen interest in improvisation. They became key players in the story of the First Studio, which therefore reads less about Stanislavsky per se and more about Stanislavsky and his collaborators.

Second, a discussion about the First Studio prompts an evaluation of the difference between improvisation and études. The latter is the term usually adopted in reference to improvised sketches used to study a scene. Generally speaking, improvisations are taken to be freer than études which, linked as they are to a text or a scene, are governed by a predetermined set of reference points which actors must follow. Anatoly Vasiliev understands the difference between the two along the same lines:

> Improvisation is freer than an etude. One can say that in an etude, an actor improvises. That would not be a mistake. But an etude is located, say, in Africa. It is always a matter of geography, of mapping the play; and we move around within the confines of that map. We are guided by the map when we improvise in an etude. But an improvisation may go entirely elsewhere! An etude allows us to study the play by means of action; the action develops in parallel with the map; we extract action from the author's text, like geography from a map. During an improvisation, however, the actor creates action from a given theme. (Vasiliev in Carnicke, 2019: 20)

A similar thinking seems to have permeated the First Studio, with Suler using impromptu events, such as acting drunk in public, 'to keep the studists on their toes' (Shevtsova, 2020: 139). Vakhtangov and Chekhov were particularly well known for these improvised jokes and pranks. Amusing though these improvisations certainly were, Vakhtangov also treated them as an opportunity to develop the actor's creative instincts and ability to resolve a task (Malaev-Babel, 2012: 82). The difference between improvisations and études is blurred when one considers that improvisation, i.e. the ability to come up with creative solutions in the moment, is the foundation of any successful étude. Thus, Mel Gordon describes études as 'directed improvisations' (1987: xiii), while Sharon Marie Carnicke

(2019: 19) refers to them as 'improvisatory explorations of their characters' circumstances and stories'; on her part, Maria Shevtsova (2020: 140) adds that 'an etude, once started, requires improvisation within the agreed framework'. It is for this reason that I use improvisation and études rather interchangeably in this section, and draw from the literature on both in my discussion.

The Studio provided Stanislavsky with a space to develop his System. It focused on the actor's craft, both individually and in an ensemble. Improvisation played a key role in this training. At the First Studio, work on improvisation can be classified as follows:

(i) as a tool to work on a technical element of the System;
(ii) in the form of Gorky's Method, i.e. as a process to create new plays;
(iii) in relation to structure and, therefore, located to performance work.

Improvising a scene not as an end in itself but to explore an element of the System was one of Suler's main contributions to the training. The aim here was not to see how far the improvisation could be taken in terms of its plot, but rather to use a scenario for a more technical and acting-based study. In a letter to Gorky, Suler wrote that he was suggesting scenarios 'depending on what I wanted to get from the students: concentration, temper, ability to communicate with a partner, ability to influence another object one way or another, and so on' (in Vinogradskaia Vol. 2 2003: 374). Examples of improvisation used for such technical training abound. A scene where a woman looks through a tram window onto her injured husband became an exercise in the circles of attention; another scene at the barber's shop was treated as an exercise in performing accurate actions (Shevtsova, 2020: 137 and 141); a slow procession to the gallows, waiting desperately for the mailman, and enjoying a meal at a station when the train unexpectedly arrives all became exercises in rhythm (Leach, 2003: 97). Training in emotional recall was also set to improvisation: 'there were improvisations and etudes aimed at sensitizing the actor to emotion: the actor was to sit by the bed of his dying father; to calm down an overwrought person; or to say goodbye in different circumstances' (88).

The application of improvisation as 'a method of training' (Evans, 2015: xxv) would become a core feature of Stanislavsky's book *An Actor's*

Work, where a scenario like that of 'the burning money' was repeatedly improvised on and features in the chapters on muscular release, belief and a sense of truth, and emotion memory (Stanislavski, 2008b)—this is a typical example of how practices first explored at the First Studio impacted Stanislavsky's later work. Improvisation can certainly be trained as a skill in its own right, but it can also be used to connect together diverse performance elements. For instance, Merlin today shows how improvisations on simple scenarios like being on top of a mountain, Sunday teatime, and a hospital waiting room draw in acting elements like adaptation, attention, and justification. More complex improvisations (by adding objectives and inner actions) involve the scaffolding of further elements like subtext and action within pauses (Merlin, 2003: 118–23), while improvisations in pairs help actors to understand and develop connections with one another.

Using improvisation to work on acting skills

Mel Gordon's collection of First Studio exercises features plenty of scenarios earmarked for the development of a particular acting skill (see especially Gordon 1987: 68 [Affective Memory] and 70 [Communication]). Rather than recount these, I will offer some original scenarios of my own that are inspired by the work of the First Studio. Users are invited to reflect on the possible acting skills or techniques which are being worked upon in each scenario. I deliberately leave this open, in the knowledge that specific exercises often lend themselves to the development of different acting skills.

- Improvise some daily routine of yours. For example, attempt in the studio the part of the day when you are preparing to leave for school or work…brush your teeth, make up the bed, prepare breakfast, collect your needs in a bag, look for the keys, switch off the lights, leave the apartment, and so on. You can also attempt the same improvisation in the actual surroundings of your own apartment. How does the improvisation and technical focus change from one space to the other?
- Identify a series of actions that involve answering a short email: open and switch on the laptop, wait for the computer to boot, access the email, read it, understand its contents and implications, and answer with a brief reply. Repeat the sequence but in different circumstances, such as (i) an invitation to a party (ii) an email from a hotel

> confirming an important, last-minute booking (iii) the possibility of a life-changing job interview.
> - Convince your scene partner of the need to make a particular purchase. It is important to define what the purchase is, and why you feel it is needed – as Stanislavsky often remarked, doing things 'in general' is the enemy of art. The partner is not really ready to spend the money, preferring instead to keep the funds for some future emergency. How is the improvisation resolved?
> - Two siblings are clearing their mother's house, who passed away recently. They find an important object from their youth, like a picture of a family holiday. What memories does the object evoke? How does it bring the two siblings closer to one another?
> - Set up the space with a number of objects. Ask participants to move from one object to the other, to hold the object in their hands, to experiment and play with it, to relate to it. How do they give value to these interactions? How do these interactions become meaningful? What makes the improvisations interesting to watch? How are shared moments, when two participants meet around one object, negotiated?

Initially, Stanislavsky articulated part of the First Studio's remit as follows: 'It exists to work on issues related to the art of acting (the System), to train an actor, to give him the opportunity to practice daily and probably in the future create parallel performances' (in Vinogradskaia Vol. 2 2003: 344). This means that even in Stanislavsky's early thinking, the Studio was not to be entirely detached from performance work, even if in that use of the word 'probably' one can sense Stanislavsky's resentment on the matter. This tug-of-war between training and performance would ultimately prove to be the Studio's undoing, with Stanislavsky begrudgingly conceding that the students' desire for performance was too strong. As a solution to the training-performance conflict, mounting productions was treated as another form of training. In this case, improvisation was again adopted as a rehearsal tool, taking forward the first discoveries that Stanislavsky had made in previous years. For example, the improvisations on technique-related elements such as affective memory and rhythm were transposed in the rehearsals for *The Wreck of the 'Hope'*, were they became embroiled in the dramaturgy of the production (Gauss, 1999: 40). Animal improvisations were also attempted (Gordon, 1987: 44).

The First Studio's use of improvisation gains in importance when it is located in the broader artistic context. One way of reading the Russian theatre tradition is by focusing on the tension between performance and literature. Which was the higher art? Which had the highest status? Is performance 'sensual' and literature 'pure' and therefore more morally uplifting? This tension was also evident at the Art Theatre, as I have mentioned briefly in the previous section when referring to the fraught relationship between Nemirovich-Danchenko and Stanislavsky. Outside the MAT, the tension remained unresolved even at the time of the Studio's opening. A debate was stirred in 1912, i.e. the year of the Studio's opening, by the publication of Yury Aikhenvald's essay titled 'The Denial of Theatre'. In this essay Aikhenvald argued for literature's higher status when compared to performance. He claimed that performance was a slave to written texts, was restricted in the meanings that it could transmit, and that it dampens the imagination of the spectator. The essay generated robust answers from theatre people like Nemirovich-Danchenko, Fyodor Komissarzhevsky, and Nikolai Evreinov, who defended the position of theatre as an art form on its own terms (Aquilina, 2020: 42).

The First Studio's contribution to these debates took the form of an experiment which came to be known as Gorky's Method. Suggested by Gorky himself in December 1910, and first recounted by Stanislavsky in a letter to Nemirovich-Danchenko in July 1912 (in Vinogradskaia Vol. 2 2003: 341), Gorky's Method involved actors improvising on outlines provided by a playwright. The latter would see and record these sketches, which he then refines and offers back to the actor for further treatment. A polished dramatic piece would thus emerge from this process between actors and author, with the director or leader also playing a part by keeping the improvisations on track. The fact that this method was not kept a secret within the walls of the Studio, but actually featured in a public article on the Studio's work (published in April 1913 in the newspaper *Russkie Vedomosti*), reads like the Studio's official statement on the performance-literature debates taking place at the time. A section of the press statement read as follows:

> The essence of this experiment, in its most general and schematic form, is as follows: a play is created together by an author and the actors. It is a result of their common work. The author gives the first push. He can be likened to the throwing of the grain in the actors' soil. The actors

then develop this grain through their own experiences, feelings, and talents. Subsequently, the author collects the harvest and gives it back to the actors. (in Vinogradskaia Vol. 2 2003: 381–382)

Not all actors were suited for this work, and Gorky underlined that participants must be resourceful and daring. They also needed a critical attitude towards that most-ingrained acting attitude, namely using the playwright's words to express one's thoughts and ideas (in Aquilina, 2020: 44). Resourcefulness, being daring, and possessing a critical mind, however, are not qualities which an actor is simply born with. In other words, improvisation helps to develop these important attitudes and to use them when developing character-work, when making important rehearsal decisions, and during performance work itself because of the interconnectedness in the actor's work. Working on improvisation, therefore, has deeper implications than simply bringing a scenario to its logical conclusion.

The project to create plays from improvisation, at a time when the number of new works at the MAT was at an all-time low, did gain some initial steam. The writer Aleksei Tolstoy expressed an interest in participating. So did Nemirovich-Danchenko, who suggested a scenario about actors living together, perhaps as a way of carving a place in the work of the Studio (in Vinogradskaia Vol. 2 2003: 349). In the end, the hoped-for repertoire did not materialise, though the experiment was far from a failure. It was essential to Stanislavsky's long term development as a theatre-maker and attempt to bring the actor, director, and playwright on a more equal footing, what elsewhere I refer to as a 'democratic levelling' between the three (Aquilina, 2020: 41–47). Some of Gorky's scenarios are also reproduced or summarised in that same volume of mine (61–62). These scenarios revolved around groups of people together, such as a family waiting for the return of a convicted father or actors in a room before an audition. Rather than repeat this material, I here give two scenarios of my own for readers to try out. Actors trying out these scenarios may even appoint a 'playwright' to record the pieces and subsequently work with them to polish the texts into fully-fledged theatre scripts.

> *Scenarios to develop scenes on*
> - A group of people sit around a fire. The setting could be either pleasant, such as a barbeque during a hot summer evening, or unpleasant, such as stranded on a desert island with little food. One person shares a big secret with the group. How do the others react? Create dramatic interest by including different and contrasting reactions.
> - A company meeting is held to discuss an important piece of news, such as: a strong competitor is opening an office or outlet nearby; the chair of the meeting received an email detailing a new and lucrative bonus package; the company is in serious financial trouble and might let some people go. How do the people at the meeting react? Make the characters as diverse as possible. For example, imagine how different the behaviour of a young ambitious upstart would be from that of a colleague who is retiring at the end of the year when the news of the company's liquidation is shared. The scene can give rise to further plot developments and improvisations, like taking the news home or clashes over clients to win the bonus, etc.

Stanislavsky did not steer singlehandedly the work of the Studio. As mentioned before, much fell on its participants. Stanislavsky's offshoots operating at the Studio give improvisation a decidedly contemporary edge. They shed light on the relationship between improvisation and structure, or freedom and discipline. Some eighty years later, Thomas Richards and Jerzy Grotowski would articulate this relationship as follows:

> High-level spontaneity can arrive only in a piece which is structured. At that point the actors can find freedom inside their structure, freedom not to change their line of actions, but to adjust slightly in reaction to one another (and to everything around), still keeping the same intentions and the same line of actions. This is some kind of subtle improvisation in which the structure is tight, and of course perfectly memorized. Grotowski stated: 'Spontaneity is impossible without structure. Rigour is necessary to have spontaneity'. (Richards 1995: 81–82)

The roots of this understanding can be traced back to the First Studio. The issue of improvisation and structure was especially raised by Michael Chekhov. A master of improvisation himself with a highly developed creative intuition, Chekhov 'goaded his partners on stage with impromptu variations and shifts of characterization—expressions, movements, actions and anything else his imagination conjured up in the moment' (Shevtsova, 2020: 140; see also Gauss, 1999: 45). This could certainly be seen as an over-indulgence on Chekhov's part, a way of showing off his talent, but his improvisations could also serve as a creative impulse for his stage partners to raise their game and answer with improvisations of their own. It all depended, in reality, on the courage and skill of his stage partners.

Chekhov's treatment of improvisation is explained in his book *To the Actor: On the Technique of Acting*. In Chapter 3 of the book, titled 'Improvisation and Ensemble', he detailed a complex exercise in improvisation which can be summarised as follows. The actor initiates the exercise by deciding on starting and concluding points for an improvisation, paying particular attention to make these as contrasting as possible. It is also important to articulate these points as clear actions, as something to be done or carried out. A mood is also chosen. These fixed points and preliminary decisions are called 'necessities', which Chekhov considers as essential details on which the actor bases his improvisation. In performance they take the form of plot, lines, contributions from the author, director, or other actors, and so on. The start and end points are fixed, but what takes place in between is improvised:

> The middle part [between the two points], the whole transition from starting to concluding points, is what you will improvise. [...] [R]eal and true freedom in improvising must always be based upon [the] necessity [of the fixed points]; otherwise it will soon degenerate into either arbitrariness or indecision. [...] Your sense of freedom would be meaningless without a place to start or without direction or destination. (Chekhov, 2002: 38–39)

Far from a free-for-all endeavour, improvisation is in this way supported by a certain amount of fixity, helping to keep it within reasonable limits. The necessities offer the structure, which the actor then 'colours' through subtext, physical actions, gestures, nuanced intonations, and so on.

Work on the improvisation is deepened by introducing a middle point and, eventually, further intermediary points that help to tighten the structure. The duration between one point and the next is also fixed with utmost precision, becoming another necessity 'to which you must accommodate yourself' (Chekhov, 2002: 40). Even within this tighter structure, the trajectory leading from one point to the next remains available for the actor to improvise on. An actor who needs thirty seconds to cross the stage would always keep this timing, for instance, but they would improvise on the manner of crossing depending on where their intuition takes them in the present moment. In this improvising the actor does not follow the behavioural logic that would become central to Stanislavsky's Method of Physical Action, i.e. the uninterrupted chain where one action logically leads to the next. Actors rather follow 'the psychological succession of inner events (feelings, emotions, wishes and other impulses)' (46), cementing further Chekhov's artistic personality as that of a highly-intuitive performer who played beyond what a director or an author might have envisaged.[5]

Improvisation was something of an overarching guideline for Vakhtangov, in a different way to Chekhov given that Vakhtangov was a director and pedagogue more than an actor.[6] Vakhtangov's understanding of improvisation revolved around what today Merlin (2023) might refer to as 'a constant state of inner improvisation'. This implies that while the score of an actor's performance is fixed and repeatable, it is rediscovered anew every night and, consequently, infused with unique psychological detail. In this sense, each performance is given a distinctive 'quality' (Merlin, 2023: 84). It was this inner improvisation that was missing from Stanislavsky's acting around 1904–06 when, in Finland, he noted that he was 'going onstage empty inside with nothing more than my external, actorish habits, with no inner fire' (Stanislavski, 2008a: 243). Vakhtangov first touched upon this understanding of improvisation when staging *The Deluge* at the Studio (1915). The improvisation of *The Deluge* was an inner improvisation, supported by the frameworks of the character and the director's mise-en-scène (Malaev-Babel, 2012: 99).

In other performances staged outside the Studio, Vakhtangov used improvisation as a rehearsal technique, to help actors find nuance in the character, to generate performance material and, curiously, as a performance style.[7] The latter was evident when he staged *Princess Turandot* at his own Vakhtangov Theatre in 1922. Andrei Malaev-Babel recounts that the actors had devoted substantial rehearsal time to experiment with physicality, with masks, pieces of costumes, props, and so on, to the extent 'that the quality of an actor was so spontaneous and light that they produced *a complete impression* upon the audience that their performances were improvised' (Malaev-Babel, 2011: 79; my emphasis). This is confirmed by Vakhtangov himself, as recounted in the rehearsal accounts prepared by his close collaborator Boris Zakhava. Note in the following quotation the considerable use of 'as if', alluding to the make-believe and imaginative nature of theatre:

> The improvisational nature of the contemporary performance does not imply an actual improvisation onstage. It implies that everything be made in advance, forged into a precise, definite, deliberate, and singular form that has been discovered through work. At the same time, this form should be delivered in such a way that the audience would perceive everything in the performance *as if* created on the spot – accidently, spontaneously, subconsciously, entirely involuntarily. The very text of the play must sound *as if* it had not been committed to memory but rather created by the actor before the audience's eyes. The main goal has been determined thus: to act *as if* it was an improvisation. (in Malaev-Babel, 2011: 290; emphasis added)

The various approaches used in *Princess Turandot* (actors stepping out of their characters, actors playing other actors, overt-use of theatrical gestures, exploration of different walks and movement patterns, play with costumes and props, etc.) were necessary 'to find the ironic style and the right technique of acting, to achieve ease and create an impression of improvisation' (in Malaev-Babel, 2011: 293). One rehearsal proceeded as follows. Vakhtangov asked the actors playing Calef and Barak to play not the characters but what they conceived to be Italian actors performing the two roles. (Note, in Vakhtangov's instruction to play like Italian actors, his nod towards commedia dell'arte.[8]) He asked the actors to improvise some lines on the spot and they did so mischievously and inventively in order to set creative obstacles for each other. This exchange between the actors was not an end in itself but was rather used to generate a sense of ease to the delivery of the actual text once it was committed to memory. The text then 'began to sound *like* an improvisation' (291; my emphasis). Direct improvisation in the performance was also possible. Actors improvised lines in performance, at one point worrying about how contemporary and topical should these be—this was, after all, 1922. Improvised lazzi, i.e. short, physical pieces, and another nod to commedia dell'arte, were also expected (293); these lazzi were also, I believe, reminiscent of the actor's stage business discussed in the First Phase, i.e. a contained micro scene within the broader macro scene on stage. Ultimately, improvisation in Vakhtangov's hands became a tool malleable to various technical and performance needs, a practice marked by openness and application. It was the foundational core of his theatre, and one of the many bridges that link modern theatre to contemporary practice.

Less talented than both Vakhtangov and Chekhov but more politically committed, Smyshlaev used improvisation to engender collective work and creativity. His main text on the subject is the book *Tekhnika obrabotki Stsenicheskogo zrelishcha* (The Technique to Process Stage Performance), published in 1921 and again in 1922, and which had done much to provoke Stanislavsky's ire (Aquilina, 2020: 74–76). Smyshlaev framed his book around collective work as a condition for creative work. It is the director's task, Smyshlaev (1922: 11) says, to cultivate this 'atmosphere of mutual trust and comradeship between the members'.[9] Despotic means where actors are treated like pawns is counter to this collective work, but improvisation was found to nourish it. In his book Smyshlaev refers to improvisation a substantial number of times. In a first instance, it is used to dramatise poems or other pieces of literature, allowing 'a play to be born here in the collective, created by a series of free improvisations, in which participants exchange words, repeat those they like most, select their favourite, [...] [and then] record the piece' (12).

Improvisation is also used to assign roles to the actors because 'the external and internal potential of an actor wanting the role can be evidenced [when improvising]' (Smyshlaev, 1922: 14).[10] Improvisations are particularly important when working on the beginning part of a play, typically Act 1, not only to explore its specific scenes, but also 'to find the general colour of the collective' (15). Études on smaller and more manageable components of a scene, the 'bit' in Stanislavskian parlance, are carried out to elaborate on the themes of the play—here, the actors rely on their words and provide new episodes from their imagination. Further études are brought closer to the author's text, not only helping the actors to learn their lines but also 'to establish in [their] souls a particular sequence of internal intentions' (21). Such improvisations are carried out during rehearsals as well as in the daily life of the actors: 'I know the desire of the first task; now, anywhere it is possible I play [corresponding] études, which my creative fantasy grounds in all the circumstances of my everyday life' (24). Improvisation also provided a foundation for the work which Smyshlaev carried out at the theatre of the Moscow Proletkult when producing an adaptation of Émile Verhaeren poem *Insurrection*, on lines that parallel our own contemporary understanding of devised theatre (Aquilina, 2021: 151–58). Smyshlaev's understanding of theatre was certainly not as developed as that of Vakhtangov or Chekhov, but his conception of improvisation is perhaps easier to grasp in practice. It is more manageable and usable, especially when applied to amateur or semi-professional work environments.

In this section I have focused on the first phase of the First Studio and its extension in the theories and practices of Chekhov, Vakhtangov, and Smyshlaev. This first phase was brought to a sad end by Suler's death in December 1916. After that, and with Vakhtangov and then Chekhov at its helm,[11] the First Studio detached itself further from its laboratory roots to become a full-fledged production house. It did so 'with honours', says Franco Ruffini, 'but also with the constraints of performance' (in Schino, 2013: 103). In fact, it is the performances that Oliver M. Sayler speaks about when discussing the work of the First Studio in his account of post-revolutionary theatre, with several pages devoted to the brilliance of productions such as *Twelfth Night* and *The Cricket on the Hearth* (Sayler, 1920: 85–90). This emphasis on the Studio's productions is reflected further in both the literature of the time (see Pavel Markov's essay in Mollica, 1989: especially 26–35) and also in that of today (cf. Tcherkasski, 2017: 86). Stanislavsky felt betrayed by this overt-desire for production work, and in 1924 he described the Studio as the 'long-standing disease in my soul' (in Senelick, 2013: 453). This was also the time when the Studio was renamed The Second Moscow Art Theatre. With this section I hope to have drawn some attention back to the First Studio's training and formation of the actor and the role which improvisation had therein. In its 'exercise madness' (Gordon, 1987: 57), the First Studio left a legacy of exercises and improvisations for the actor to try out even today. In addition, and perhaps even more impactful, it was to leave *an improvisational frame of mind* which, through the international movement of Stanislavsky's collaborators and students, was to appear, in different guises and under different names, in many theatre realities around the world.[12]

Notes

1. Stanislavsky soon understood the need to train every new generation of actors. The Second Studio was founded in 1916; its members replenished the main house and reached maturation in the production of *The Days of the Turbins* (1926). The Third Studio was founded in 1920 and eventually became known as The Vakhtangov Theatre. The Fourth Studio was more of an outreach group tasked with taking theatre to the workers. Other studios

associated with Stanislavsky are the Bolshoi Opera Studio and the Opera-Dramatic Studio. For a chart and summary of Stanislavsky's various studio endeavours see Shevtsova (2020: 129–31).

2. Pavel Markov's definition of pedagogy in the context of the First Studio is particularly clear: 'Theatre pedagogy does not only provide training in a specific technique. It also serves to discover a particular idea' (in Mollica, 1989: 17). All translations from Italian are mine.

3. At the Art Theatre, young beginners were typically casted in minor roles and crowd scenes.

4. Mel Gordon (1987: 42) for instance says the following when discussing Suler and the broader moral tendencies of the Studio: 'The new actor, who relies on truth and experience for his expression and inspiration, could expose—and therefore change—the everyday world of lies'.

5. Chekhov's exercise in improvisation can also be performed in a group, where any small hint from the partner or partners—a shift of the eyes, a tiny gesture or movement, an unexpected intonation, and so on—serves as an impulse to take the improvisation forward. Generally speaking, group improvisations need to be more detailed, with more initial necessities (theme, setting, parts, etc.) so as to ground participants together in the same improvisatory space. The general plot and succession of events are, however, to be developed during the improvisation (Chekhov, 2002: 43).

6. In fact, that was exactly Stanislavsky's initial assessment of Vakhtangov (Benedetti, 1999: 210). The First Studio also accelerated its transformation into a production house when, following Suler's death, Vakhtangov was appointed its director.

7. On Vakhtangov use of improvisation in rehearsal see Malaev-Babel (2011: 262 and 270).

8. On Vakhtangov's interpretation and application of commedia dell'arte see Vazzoler (2018: 258–60).

9. I will quote further from Smyshlaev's book given that there is no English translation. Smyshlaev further describes collective creativity as follows: 'The essence and secret of theatre art is in its collectivism, in the 'community' of action, in the friendly comradely solidarity of all the individuals working in the collective, beginning with the workers driving in the nails into the decorations and

ending with the director composing the creative work of theatre art.' (Smyshlaev, 1922: 11).
10. Smyshlaev continues to write as follows: 'While serving to identify one or more of the play's participants, the main aim of these improvisations is to open up the soul on which the seeds of the author's desires will be sown. These sketches are the first sector in the creative circle and in the search for an artistic stage work.' (Smyshlaev, 1922: 14).
11. Vakhtangov would himself pass prematurely in 1922.
12. Michael Chekhov, with his teaching at Dartington and work in American cinema, easily comes to mind (see Chamberlain, 2004: 26–34). On the international dissemination of improvisation within the context of the Stanislavsky acting tradition see some examples in Pitches and Aquilina (2017: 90, 154, 226, 241, 262, and 301).

References

Aquilina, S. (2020). *Modern theatre in Russia: Tradition building and transmission processes*. Bloomsbury.
Aquilina, S. (Ed.). (2021). *Amateur and proletarian theatre in post-revolutionary Russia: Primary sources*. Bloomsbury.
Benedetti, J. (1999). *Stanislavski: His life and art*. Methuen.
Carnicke, S. (2019). Improvisations and etudes: An experiment in Active Analysis. *Stanislavski Studies, 7*(1), 17–35.
Chamberlain, F. (2004). *Michael Chekhov*. Routledge.
Chekhov, M. (2002). *To the actor: On the technique of acting*. Routledge.
Evans, M. (Ed.). (2015). *The actor training reader*. Routledge.
Gauss, R. (1999). *Lear's daughters*. Peter Lang.
Gordon, M. (1987). *The Stanislavsky technique: Russia*. Applause.
Leach, R. (2003). *Stanislavsky and Meyerhold*. Peter Lang.
Malaev-Babel, A. (Ed.). (2011). *The Vakhtangov sourcebook*. Routledge.
Malaev-Babel, A. (2012). *Yevgeny Vakhtangov: A critical portrait*. Routledge.
Merlin, B. (2003). *Konstantin Stanislavsky*. Routledge.
Merlin, B. (2023). Hear, now, today: Active Analysis for the working actor A "special guest workshop" delivered at the S Word, Prague, 12 November 2022. *Stanislavski Studies, 11*(1), 81–98.
Mollica, F. (Ed.) (1989) *Il teatro possibile*. La Casa Usher.
Pitches, J., & Aquilina, S. (Eds.). (2017). *Stanislavsky in the world: The system and its transformations across continents*. Bloomsbury.

Richards, T. (1995). *At work with Grotowski on physical actions.* Routledge.
Sayler, O. M. (1920). *The Russian theatre under the revolution.* Little, Brown and Company.
Schino, M. (2013). *Alchemists of the stage: Theatre laboratories in Europe.* Icarus Publishing Enterprise.
Senelick, L. (Ed. and trans.) (2013) *Stanislavsky: His life in letters.*
Shevtsova, M. (2020). *Rediscovering Stanislavsky.* Cambridge University Press.
Smyshlaev, V. (1922). *Tekhnika obrabotki Stsenicheskogo zrelishcha [The technique to process stage performance]* (2nd ed.). All-Russian Proletkult.
Stanislavski, K. (2008a) *My life in art.* (J. Benedetti, Trans.). Routledge.
Stanislavski, K. (2008b) *An actor's work* (J. Benedetti, Trans.). Routledge.
Tcherkasski, S. (2017). Forward—to early Stanislavsky! or reconstruction of actor training at the first studio of the Moscow Art Theatre. *Stanislavski Studies, 5*(1), 85–110.
Vazzoler, F. (2018). Staging Gozzi: Meyerhold, Vakhtangov, Brecht, Besson. In C. B. Balme, P. Vescovo, & D. Vianello (Eds.), *Commedia dell'Arte in context* (pp. 254–65). Cambridge University Press.
Vinogradskaia, I. N. (2003) *Zhizn i tvorchestvo K. S. Stanislavskogo.* [The Life and Work of K. S. Stanislavsky, 4 volumes]. Moscow Art Theatre Press.

CHAPTER 5

Fourth Phase: 1924–28 and Stanislavsky's Final Legacies of the 1930s

Abstract Stanislavsky's approaches to directing in the mid-to-late 1920s and the role improvisation played therein are discussed. A key concern for Stanislavsky during this politically significant time was the interpretation of a piece, which in theatre terms revolves around the identification of a throughaction that traverses a play and performance. The one key work aspect that was resolved through improvisation was the creation of the mise-en-scène. It was, however, a very different mise-en-scène from the one that had made Stanislavsky's reputation as a highly creative director. By now he was totally committed to an actor's theatre, which meant that the mise-en-scène was less fixed and more fluid, emerging from the improvisations of the actors on the actual stage, late in the rehearsal process, and when they encountered sets, props, furniture arrangements, and so on. The chapter identifies these improvisations, rooted as they were in the actor's 'here, today, now', as a key stepping stone towards Active Analysis and Stanislavsky's final legacies.

Keywords Throughaction · Rehearsal · Active Analysis · Here, today, now · Maria Knebel · Improvisation

The year 1917 was a tumultuous one for Stanislavsky and the country at large when a three-centuries old dynasty was brought down by the

February Revolution. A Provisional Government headed first by Georgy Lvov and then by Alexander Kerensky followed, but this proved to be short-lived as the October Revolution and the Bolshevik Party spearheaded a bloody civil war. Stanislavsky lost his fortune and his home—he would eventually be relocated to an apartment on Leontievski Lane—with the ensuing years devoted more to opera, pedagogy, and to the occasional production as he slowly adjusted himself to a very different life, a new world, the rising avant-garde, and a new role within the Art Theatre and the theatrical landscape at large.[1] In this section, I will focus on what I feel is the next important phase of Stanislavsky, that between 1924 and 1928. I came to believe that these years are Stanislavsky's 'largely forgotten years'. There are huge chunks of work in these years which simply rarely feature in contemporary scholarship.[2] The reason I give for this is that these years are sandwiched between two major milestones in Stanislavsky's career, milestones which tend to hog a lot of scholarly limelight. These are the 1922–24 international tours, especially the American ones, which were responsible for his international reputation, and the experiments of the 1930s in physical action and Active Analysis, which came to receive the accolade of Stanislavsky's 'final legacies'.

That we tend to somehow side-line his 1924–28 work is even more inconceivable to me given the renewed energy with which Stanislavsky returned to production work and to the Moscow Art Theatre itself. This surprising return to action was at least partially motivated by the fact that Nemirovich-Danchenko left Moscow in October 1925 with a tour of his Music Studio—without Nemirovich-Danchenko's incessant drive to control the MAT, Stanislavsky experienced a second youth. And it was with the young that he surrounded himself again, not only with younger actors, such as those of the Second Studio who at this time were incorporated in the main house, but also with young directors and collaborators. Key among the latter were Ilya Sudakov and Pavel Markov who, though certainly independent artists in their own right, were sympathetic to Stanislavsky's understanding of theatre. By now the System had also generally become the working method of the MAT, meaning that Stanislavsky could offload a substantial amount of preparatory work on the other directors, for him to come in at key moments to correct, amend, and provide fresh direction as needed (Benedetti, 1999: 299). This allowed him the possibility to work on a staggering number of new productions during this period, some 9 dramatic pieces and 5 operas in fact.[3]

5 FOURTH PHASE: 1924–28 AND STANISLAVSKY'S FINAL ... 55

When working on these productions, Stanislavsky's use of improvisation was not as overt as it was in previous years, though it did not disappear altogether. With one notable exception in the creation of the mises-en-scène which I will discuss here, the sources that I consulted make a scantier reference to improvisation. Stanislavsky certainly continued to improvise demonstrations in rehearsal when these were absolutely necessary or when an opening night was near and thus quick results were required.[4] One of his own roles, that of Famusov in *Woe from Wit*, appeared essentially improvised, at least to the eyes of Nikolai Gorchakov, another young director at the MAT. Stanislavsky's intonations, Gorchakov remarked, 'were unusually expressive. They changed from performance to performance, and it was quite obvious that Stanislavsky did not prepare them in advance, but that they were born on stage from those incidents of the current performance that he loved to use' (in Vinogradskaia Vol. 3 2003: 368).

One other documented instance of Stanislavsky's use of improvisation during these years has a very particular setting. On the 9 April 1925, Stanislavsky guested at the State Academic Drama Theatre (formerly the Alexandrinsky) for a rehearsal and a one-off performance of *Woe from Wit*, in which he reappraised his role of Famusov. With only a few hours set aside to rehearse with the cast, Stanislavsky opted to try and revitalise the crowd scenes. He divided the actors in pairs, and asked them to come up with a topic for a private conversation. No over-thinking was required, as Stanislavsky wanted the pairs to dialogue on the first thing that came to their mind. On cue, all pairs started their improvised dialogues, which added a degree of freshness to a scene which, devoid of written lines on which actors rely, had become stale. As A. Pergament, chronicler of the rehearsal, wrote, 'for the first time, instead of "what do I say when I have nothing to say", some living words began to sound' (in Vinogradskaia Vol. 3 2003: 376). Stanislavsky then created different rhythms to the dialogue depending on the intensity of the scene. What a pity, Pergament remarked, that while in the course of those two hours Stanislavsky breathed new life into the mass scene, the troupe quickly returned to their old ways once he left. Pergament's tone seems to condemn the actors for their withdrawal to tried-and-tested routines and general laziness, but let's also remember that Stanislavsky's input was, essentially, a one-off rehearsal and experience for the actors. Improvisation, like all the other elements of the Stanislavsky System, requires constant application and practise in order to become ingrained in the actors and second nature to them.

That in these years there is less reference to improvisation can be explained by the fact that, as a director working on producing theatre, what preoccupied Stanislavsky most was the interpretation of the play and of the performance as a whole. This was especially the case given that in the 1920s, with the Soviet state consolidating itself and Stalin's rise to power, matters of *political* interpretation held paramount importance. Laurence Senelick (2013: 452), in fact, frames these years in terms of '[a]djusting to a Soviet world'. Stanislavsky was also unimpressed by the achievements of the avant-garde, the 'leftists' movements like the cubists and expressionists whom he criticised over what he felt were unjustified forms devoid of inner content—at one point he even referred to them as 'singers without meaning' (Vinogradskaia Vol. 3 2003: 476).[5] In Stanislavsky's theatre, matters of interpretation are resolved by the identification of the throughaction that traverses a play and a performance.[6] The throughaction is a play's overall concept, its 'overarching or governing idea' (Shevtsova, 2020: 177). It unifies together the various moments of a play as well as the stories of the various characters, their own throughactions so to speak. The throughaction may be initially defined in rational terms, though the key to a production process is its embodiment into a series of logical and engaging actions that provide the performance of the play its forward momentum.

Finding, consolidating, and embodying the throughline emerges as Stanislavsky's key approach during these years, the essence of his working method. Benedetti (1999: 302) makes this very clear: 'It was therefore problems of the through-action both of individual characters and of the action, of dramatic rhythm, tempo, that occupied him most'. Examples of Stanislavsky's search for the throughaction abound in the literature. Thus, for instance, when rehearsing *Woe from Wit* in December 1924 he was careful to underscore the theme of patriotism and the overall interpretation of the piece as a 'progressive, freedom-loving, high comedy' (Vinogradskaia Vol. 3 2003: 358). Discussions about the interpretation of a piece took place from the start of the rehearsal process, as evidenced by the process of *The Marriage of Figaro*.[7] This was Stanislavsky's only production of the time and the last to be credited solely to him, for which he shared his thoughts on the play during the very first meeting with the cast in August 1925. These thoughts 'formed the basis of the coming work: the super-objective of the performance and the throughline of the action of the play' (Vinogradskaia Vol. 3 2003: 396). Some of this work was carried out at the table, as evidenced during another

Figaro rehearsal dated 16 October 1925,[8] and another for *Les Merchands de Gloire* dated 1 June 1926 (455). *Les Merchands de Gloire* opened a fortnight later to highlight further the prolonged gestation period of the throughline, which could take a long time to mature and for the actors to come to terms with. Ultimately, the throughline could make a production's success or prove its undoing. The latter was the fate of Aeschylus' *Prometheus*, which had been in rehearsal for more than a year when Stanislavsky cancelled the production because he believed that it did not speak to the modern spectator.[9]

One particularly side-lined performance of these years was the production of Aleksandr Ostrovsky's *A Burning Heart*.[10] The play opened in January 1926 and it quickly established itself as a major success for both Stanislavsky and the Art Theatre. The production was Stanislavsky's answer to Anatoly Lunacharsky's 'Return to Ostrovsky' policy, which made matters of interpretation even more acute.[11] The interpretation of this nineteenth-century play again revolved around making the production speak to a modern, contemporary audience. Far from politically naïve, Stanislavsky appeared highly conversant with the class issues of the play. In a rehearsal dated 27 October 1925, he 'spoke about the need to identify more clearly and to develop the line of positive characters, which in the acts shown was pale and inexpressive' (Vinogradskaia Vol. 3 2003: 405). A day later he strove to sharpen the distinction between the positive characters and dark kingdom depicted in the play. A note describing another rehearsal dated 5 December 1925 says that Stanislavsky 'spoke to the performers about the interpretation of this or that scene' (413). Other rehearsals at the table carried out on the 10 and 16 December furthered strengthened the performers' understanding of their lines (Vinogradskaia Vol. 3 2003: 414 and 415). Even at a dress rehearsal in January 1926, it was the ideological meaning of the production that mattered most to Stanislavsky, as evidenced by the all-important rehearsal feedback that he gave to the cast: 'In conversation with the performers, he remarked that the theme of the play's positive heroes, the theme of the struggle for human dignity, for the rights of the common man, has not yet been revealed sufficiently and vividly enough' (Vinogradskaia Vol. 3 2003: 421).[12]

Given Stanislavsky's emphasis on matters of interpretation and their embodiment in stage action, it is conceivable to think that his use of improvisation took a back seat. In fact, the one key work aspect of the time that was resolved through improvisation was the creation of the mise-en-scène. It was, however, a very different mise-en-scène to the one that had made Stanislavsky's reputation as a highly creative director. By now he was totally committed to an actor's theatre,[13] which meant that the mise-en-scène was less fixed and much more fluid, emerging from the improvisations of the actors on the actual stage when they encountered sets, props, furniture arrangements, etc. As discussed in the Second Phase, in his directorial work Stanislavsky created the mise-en-scène first before the actual work with the actors started. He then used the rehearsals with the cast to translate his ideas from the written page to the stage. His approach in the 1920s would be diametrically opposite: evidence shows that he left the improvised discovery of a mise-en-scène very late in the rehearsal process. For example, at least some of the mises-en-scène for *Nicholas I and the Decembrists* were discovered just 10 days before opening night. Their construction 'proceeded from the inner content of the performers' (Vinogradskaia Vol. 3 2003: 446) rather than his personal invention, highlighting further Stanislavsky's focus on the actor.

A person who entered Stanislavsky's last years of work was none other than Maria Knebel, the main collaborator at his final Opera-Dramatic Studio (1935–38) and torchbearer for his final improvisatory approach which, thanks to her endeavours, came to be known as Active Analysis. Knebel came to the theatre via Michael Chekhov, who was her first teacher and, like many others, was impressed by his talent for improvisation.[14] She joined the Art Theatre in 1924, after an apprenticeship of some years at the Second Studio.[15] Her autobiography *Vsia Zhizn'* (The Whole Life) is important not only as a summary of her artistic life but also because she documents several rehearsals with Stanislavsky. Given that she was writing from the point of a view of an actress and a director, i.e. a practitioner, her writings are particularly rich with practical details of Stanislavsky's work.

In one such description of the rehearsals for *Figaro*, Knebel described Stanislavsky's approach to creating crowd scenes which, she says, he still held high in esteem as a theatrical device. Gone were the minute details created by the director for the actors to follow blindly. His approach to creating mass scenes was as far removed from these authoritarian ways as one can possibly imagine, with Knebel saying that Stanislavsky 'constructed the crowd scenes in an improvisatory manner' (in Knebel, 1967: 241). In *Figaro* Knebel only had a small part to play, that of an old woman in the crowd scenes. Stanislavsky liked her creation and, building on Knebel's prompt, constructed a mini-group of four such characters.

In the trial scene, the four actresses were tasked with sticking together. On lines which Knebel would subsequently make central in Active Analysis, Stanislavsky also introduced an obstacle or counteraction for them to overcome, namely that younger members in the crowd were to try and separate the old women and make them sit in different places of the room. Knebel writes as follows:

> We were separated, but we wanted to share our impressions with each other all the time. Every now and then we jumped up and explained ourselves with glances and gestures. This created one of those countless colours that gave the mass scene of the play an amazing liveness. (Knebel, 1967: 241).

Stanislavsky's approach as a director emerges from this last anecdote. Rather than suggesting solutions to the actors, he restricted himself to offering tasks, or structures (in this case an objective, and an action and counteraction), for the four actresses to improvise solutions on. It is an actor's theatre, for sure, but one in which the actor and director are in a creative and supportive relationship. Like he did during the Second Phase when improvising in Gorky's Method, the figure of the director is transformed rather than negated. It remains to polish the actors' improvisations within the overarching montage of a scene, episode, act, or even the performance as a whole. To achieve this final polish, Stanislavsky took on the role of an editor:

> Bright, unexpected mises-en-scènes arose because he knew how to interest everyone in what was happening, not allowing us to forget for a minute the individual characteristics. [...] Giving us a lot of initiative at the beginning [when improvising], Stanislavsky then selected everything that was necessary, discarding the unnecessary. (Knebel, 1967: 241)

Another crowd scene in *Figaro* took place during a wedding. Knebel describes this scene as one of the most remarkable moments of the production, where 'everything was new, unexpected, bright, strikingly flowing, and a complete unity of the author, director, artist, and actors. As in other mass scenes, everything began with an improvisation' (Knebel 1967: 243). In this case the improvisation involved the presentation of a bouquet of flowers and the singing of a comical song by the old women, which Stanislavsky took advantage of and presumably kept in the production. The use of improvisation to create the mise-en-scène clearly became a recurring method in the production process, with Knebel saying that she 'got used to the fact that Stanislavsky built his magnificent mises-en-scène improvisationally—he directed us and delivered his corrections from the audience' (Knebel 1967: 303). Keeping in mind the conclusions reached above when discussing Vakhtangov and Chekhov, Stanislavsky's understanding of improvisation in these years was at its most developed. He created structures to facilitate the actor's improvisatory (creative) state, as Knebel explains in the most succinct of manners: 'The text, the precision of relationships, even the mise-en-scène, are the unshakable foundation on which the actor improvises. In what is the actor free? In his solutions, in the colours [of the role], in the subtext' (Knebel, 1967: 62).

In October 1928 the Moscow Art Theatre celebrated its twenty-year jubilee with a series of extracts from some of its most famous works. Stanislavsky appeared as Vershinin in Act One of *Three Sisters*, when he suffered a near-fatal heart attack (Benedetti, 1999: 317). This brought an end to his acting career, and after that day Stanislavsky understood that he was living on borrowed time. The last ten years of his life were punctuated by regular treatments and convalesces, sometimes abroad, even if his theatrical instincts remained very much alive, especially when it came to pedagogy and other studio work carried out in the comfort (and surveillance) of his own personal apartment. As Senelick (2013: 500) says on the years that followed, 'the bulk of the MAAT productions would be staged by Nemirovich-Danchenko, with the occasional contribution by Sudakov and others. KS would devise, supervise or touch up a particular work, but almost never ran rehearsals in the theatre'. This makes the records of Stanislavsky's rehearsals for the production of Aleksandr Ostrovsky's *Artists and Admirers* (1933) even more valuable. This production again rarely features in contemporary scholarship about Stanislavsky, although I have made it a point to bring his work on it to light (Aquilina, 2012a, 2013, 2016, and 2020: 47–53). Rehearsals for *Artists and Admirers* started in March 1932 under the direction of N. N. Litovtseva. Stanislavsky became involved in the production in December, and the play opened on the 23 September 1933. In total he contributed to some 18 rehearsals.

The main rehearsal notes are not entirely devoid of improvisation. There are two references, dated 7 and 23 March, which taken together exhibit Stanislavsky's thinking about the improvisatory nature of performance. During the second rehearsal he talked to the actors about the logic of the actions, and how each task is divided into a series of smaller and then even smaller and more manageable components, not for them to remain fragmented but to help the actor rediscover an organicity and flow to the role. One danger of this fragmentation is that the score of physical actions (e.g. turning a door knob, opening the door, looking around the room, entering, and finding one's place in the room) becomes a dead, technical endeavour without any inner life, a recall of the 'technical gymnastics' which Stanislavsky felt his seminal role of Dr Stockman in *An Enemy of the People* (1900) had developed into after a few years of performance (Stanislavski, 2008: 260). Stanislavsky's never forgot past lessons, as he endeavoured to create ever new ways to keep the role fresh and alive for, first and foremost, the actor. This, he believed, would also benefit the audience.

In the 1930s, Stanislavsky again turned to improvisation as a way of keeping the role alive. During the rehearsals for *Artists and Admirers* he argued that whereas issues related to where, when, and why (collected together under the 'what') must indeed be 'secured as hard and as in depth as possible' (Vinogradskaia, 2000: 242), the actual action-based way of accomplishing the task, i.e. the 'how', should be left to spontaneity and improvisation (this, I believe, is what Knebel meant with the use of the word 'devices'—*prisposobleniyakh*—above). The 'how', he emphasised, should be left to the subconscious to handle. To keep with the previous example of entering the room, an actor working in this way would have several ways of scanning the room, for example, or several options in moving to the chosen spot. On each night the actors would then choose, i.e. improvise, from among these options depending on his creative instincts. As Stanislavsky says, '*[s]pontaneity and improvisation on the stage is what best of all refreshes the role and breathes new life into it*' (242; emphasis in the original). This assertion, italicised in the notes for added emphasis, builds on a similar statement Stanislavsky had made during the 7 March rehearsal:

> An artistic theatre has to make the audience want to visit Negina's apartment more than once. However, to achieve this we must always be living for today, not simply repeating yesterday's gestures and intonations. *The repetition of methods kills the role and dries up the play. Your acting must always be half-improvised.* (Vinogradskaia, 2000: 233; emphasis in the original).

That these statements are given in italics is not an insignificant detail. Presented as such, they are elevated beyond a specific moment of rehearsal and rendered into transferable techniques that can be applied to a variety of contexts (Aquilina, 2020: 49–51). An approach to improvisation that is based on structure and spontaneity thus becomes one such transferable principle, possible across different performance realities and irrespective of style or genre.

Mises-en-scène for *Artists and Admirers* were worked out in two rehearsals dated 14 and 16 May 1933. The rehearsals were documented by Boris Zon, who was then studying with Stanislavsky as a participant in his home research (Shevtsova, 2020: 140). *Artists and Admirers* revolves around Negina, a provincial actress dreaming of a theatre career, her various admirers, and a love triangle. A part of the action takes place in her private apartment, which was first revealed to the actors during these rehearsals. The set received Stanislavsky's approval, as it corresponded with the models that he had previously seen. Costumes and make-up were also tried on, with some alterations carried out in order to simplify the designs. Additions like large noses, which Stanislavsky deemed 'too grotesque', were removed. These, he argued, were only needed 'when the role lacks an internal design' (Vinogradskaia, 2000: 246).

The formation of actor groupings was attempted next. Given that the actors were now working not in a rehearsal room but on the actual stage, and on the set of Negina's apartment, any previous mises-en-scène were abandoned. They needed to be found anew. The actors were asked to take the stage and inhabit it as actors first, then as the characters. They did this by reacting spontaneously to their surroundings: they walked, touched things, leant against furniture, handled props, and so on. In her introduction to the rehearsal notes, Vinogradskaia emphasised the improvisatory and spontaneous nature of this exercise and the sense of exploration which now governed rehearsals:

> When working for several months with the performers of *Artists and Admirers*, Stanislavsky did not say anything about the mise-en-scène. To be more precise, he suggested that the actors should not tie themselves to a particular mise-en-scène. This was central to his new method of work, for which one of the most important conditions was the internal freedom of the actor and improvisation during the moments of creativity. Stanislavsky started work on the mise-en-scène only towards the last period of rehearsals, when the decorations were installed on the stage and the

make-up and costumes were approved. The stage director gave the actors the opportunity to choose their own place on the stage—where to stand, sit, where to move, etc. Actors were asked to come in and look around their new surroundings to get a more comfortable and lively positioning. (Vinogradskaia, 2000: 212)

The same improvisatory work was carried out between the actors to find connections with one another. They gravitated towards and away from each other depending on the given circumstances and the inner designs of their roles. Stanislavsky noted the most interesting arrangements, which he then worked technically on, i.e. polished, by making sure, for example, that the groupings could be seen from different angles (Vinogradskaia, 2000: 247). These rehearsals to find the mises-en-scène took place only when the actors had rehearsed the piece for about fourteen months, and when they were therefore secure in their inner work, their throughlines, and overall interpretation of the piece and its characters. The previous work carried out offered a solid foundation for the actors to improvise on.

In his memoirs of the *Figaro* rehearsals, the actor B. I. Vershilov wrote as follows:

> Stanislavsky did not fix the mises-en-scène for a very long time. He wanted them to come from the actors, to be born anew each time, *'here, today, now'*. In the last act, all the performers came out on the stage and, at Stanislavsky's instruction, acted in the given circumstances and in the given rhythm. The actors ran around, collided, got entangled with each other, and Stanislavsky, who took part in these games, also got entangled with them. Gradually, he chose and remembered the most successful groupings, which served as a guide for new discoveries. (in Vinogradskaia Vol. 3 2003: 517; emphasis added).

A similar degree of 'here, today, now' is evident in the rehearsals concerning the mises-en-scène of *Artists and Admirers*, with Stanislavsky valuing unexpected moments in the actor's work as they emerged in the present, in specific moments of rehearsal (Aquilina, 2020: 52). Concealed here are very tangible steps taken by Stanislavsky towards his final, improvisation-led approach of Active Analysis, where actors were encouraged to acknowledge the reality of a situation at hand, combine it with a sense of playfulness, and improvise their way towards their own interpretation and embodiment of a text. More than any other version of his

System, it is when developing Active Analysis that he (and later Knebel), equipped with a career worth of experience of how improvisation works, formulated a rehearsal approach fully steeped in the actors' predisposition towards and skill in improvisation.

Using improvisation to create a crowd scene
- Try this exercise with the largest number of participants possible, say twenty or more. Divide the group in smaller units of 3 or 4 actors. The following scenario can be used to improvise a crowd scene on. The setting is a surprise birthday party, and the group are waiting for the arrival of the celebrant. Set up the stage accordingly, with a bar, some glasses, bottles, and nibbles, a sofa, some chairs, a small table, a window, a door, some ornaments, and so on.
- Actors improvise the scene. They move around the stage, get into groups, take or share a drink, chat, check the watch, wait, send messages, etc. They also improvise subtler behaviour, such as making eye-contact across the room, or using body language to share meaning and character traits.
- As a director or facilitator of the scene, suggest instructions (i.e. obstacles or counteractions) to enliven the scene. For example: wait, where is the cake? Or: Oh no, there is a power cut! Someone approaches you, but you are not interested.
- Your task as a director engaged in creating the mise-en-scène of this group scene is similar to what Stanislavsky experienced, i.e. 'select everything that is necessary, while discarding the unnecessary'.
- What are the criteria that dictate these choices? Balance in the visual composition of the scene? Different status between the characters? Contrasting rhythms? Overall harmony?
- Using a soft voice, side coach actors in their improvisations. For example, alert actors if they are moving too quickly from one grouping or solution to the other, or of some promising moments that were quickly discarded.
- Extend the improvisation to the moment when the celebrant arrives. How do different characters react to this moment? Compose the moment of 'Surprise!' through the various reactions offered by the actors. Also extend the scene, and the method described above, to the actual party.

NOTES

1. On Stanislavsky's reactions to the Revolution and adaptation to the new world see: Aquilina (2012b), Benedetti (1999: 245–254), Shevtsova (2020: 57–66).
2. Benedetti covers the years in 2 chapters; Shevtsova (2020: 211–218) does well to include an extended piece on *The Marriage of Figaro* in her 'rediscovery' of Stanislavsky. Beyond these sources, however, I see quite a dearth of material, which creates areas of scholarship awaiting discovery.
3. The productions are: *A Burning Heart* (Ostrovski), *Il Matrimonio Segreto* (Cimarosa), *Nicholas I and the Decembrists* (Kugel), *Les Merchands de Gloire* (Pagnol/Nivoix), *The Days of the Turbins* (Bulgakov), *The Tsar's Bride* (Rimski-Korsakov), *La Bohème* (Puccini), *The Marriage of Figaro* (Beaumarchais), *Les Soeurs Gérard* (Ennery and Cormon), *Armoured Train 14–69* (Ivanov), *May Night* (Rimski-Korsakov), *Untilovsk* (Leonov), *Boris Godunov* (Moussorgski) and *The Embezzlers* (Kataiev). See Benedetti (1999: 388). Given the politically charged period, much attention is typically invested on the production of *The Days of the Turbins* (see, for example, Benedetti, 1999: 300–04).
4. See one example when rehearsing *Untilovsk*, in Vinogradskaia (Vol. 4 2003: 9).
5. Stanislavsky shared his critical judgement on the avant-garde during a speech given at the Rostov University while on a tour of Soviet cities in 1925. I. Berezark, a member of the audience, recounted that 'Stanislavsky very vividly spoke about how the most sophisticated form, not connected with a great idea, with deep content, leads art to ruin' (Vinogradskaia Vol. 3 2003: 476). Stanislavsky was particularly disparaging of the avant-garde, as he made it clear in his evaluation of post-revolutionary theatre at the end of *My Life in Art* (Stanislasvki, 2008: 343–49). This criticism extended to the Second and Third Studios, who according to Stanislavsky had succumbed to 'futurist follies' (in Senelick, 2013: 455).
6. Throughaction is Shevtsova's preferred translation of the Russian term *skvoznoye deystviye* (Shevtsova, 2020: 232). Carnicke translates this as through-action or through line of action (Carnicke 2009: 226).

7. The full name given to this production was *A Mad Day or The Marriage of Figaro*.
8. An entry in the rehearsal diary of *Figaro* says as follows: 'We were going over the first act at the table, looking for bits, tasks, recalling how the [character's] day flows, looking for relationships with each other' (Vinogradskaia Vol. 3 2003: 402). On Stanislavsky's interpretation of the main characters in the play see Benedetti (1999: 307).
9. *Prometheus* had been in rehearsal since March 1925. It was placed under the direction of Valentin Smyshlaev. Rehearsals in April were meant to 'clarify the ideological side of the play' (Vinogradskaia Vol. 3 2003: 375). By November 1926 the work on the piece was clearly failing; in a rehearsal Stanislavsky was quoted saying that the material shown to him 'cannot satisfy the modern spectator, who now knows how to evaluate a work "from a political point of view". The modern spectator must be shown how in Greece people dream of culture. Among them appeared a revolutionary—Promethues—who wanted to bring them a spark of the divine's fire of knowledge' (500). This is when Stanislavsky decided to call off the production (Senelick, 2013: 483).
10. Benedetti only warrants the play one paragraph.
11. Concerned about the tepid state of the post-revolutionary repertoire, Lunacharsky had urged dramatists to take Ostrovsky's penchant for social criticism as a model going forward. See, amongst many other sources, Braun (1998: 205).
12. The final rehearsals of *Les Merchands de Gloire* in April 1926 were similarly devoted to the overall interpretation of the piece, 'to clarifying and sharpening the ideological ring of the play, striving to reveal more vividly the satire on the modern bourgeoisie' (Vinogradskaia Vol. 3 2003: 528).
13. His commitment to an actor's theatre was particularly evident when he expressed concern about the publication of *The Seagull*'s mise-en-scène. In the end he did give his permission, but only if the following was included in the foreword: 'Bear in mind that the mises-en-scène of *The Seagull* were made according to old, now utterly discarded methods of the enforced imposition of one's own personal feelings on to the actor, and not according to the new method of a preliminary study of the actor, his attributes, the material for his role, in order to create a mise-en-scène that will suit him

and be useful to him. In other words, the method of the old mises-en-scène belongs to the despotic director, against whom I now lead the fight, while the new mises-en-scène are made by directors who submit to the actor.' (Senelick, 2013: 462).
14. Sharon Marie Carnicke (2010: 102) writes as follows: 'He [Chekhov] taught her [Knebel] creative ways to develop her imagination through theatrical improvisations'.
15. For a much more detailed biography about Knebel see Carnicke (2010: 101–06) and Carnicke (2023: 50–68).

REFERENCES

Aquilina, S. (2012a). Stanislavski's accumulative practice in *Artists and Admirers* rehearsals (1932–33). *Stanislavski Studies*, 2, 3–20.
Aquilina, S. (2012b). Stanislavski's encounter with the Revolution. *Studies in Theatre and Performance*, 32(1), 79–91.
Aquilina, S. (2013). Stanislavski and the tactical potential of everyday images. *Theatre Research International*, 38(3), 229–39.
Aquilina, S. (2016). As simple but as complex as everyday cooking: Stanislavski's use of physical action in the recreation of nature. *Stanislavski Studies*, 4(2), 111–24.
Aquilina, S. (2020). *Modern theatre in Russia: Tradition building and transmission processes*. Bloomsbury.
Benedetti, J. (1999). *Stanislavski: His life and Art*. Methuen.
Braun, E. (1998). *Meyerhold: A revolution in theatre*. Methuen.
Carnicke, S. (2009). *Stanislavsky in Focus*, 2nd ed. Routledge.
Carnicke, S. (2010). The Knebel technique: Active Analysis in practice. In A. Hodge (Ed.), *Actor training* (pp. 99–116). Routledge.
Carnicke, S. (2023). *Dynamic acting through Active Analysis*. Bloomsbury Publishing.
Knebel, M. O. (1967). *Vsia Zhizn'* (The whole life), edited by N. A. Krymova. WTO.
Senelick, L. (Ed. and trans.) (2013). *Stanislavsky: His life in letters*.
Shevtsova, M. (2020). *Rediscovering Stanislavsky*. Cambridge University Press.
Stanislavski, K. (2008). *My life in art* (J. Benedetti, Trans.). Routledge.
Vinogradskaia, I. (Ed.). (2000). *Stanislavski Repetiruiet [Stanislavsky Rehearsing]*. Moscow Art Theatre.
Vinogradskaia, I. N. (2003). *Zhizn i tvorchestvo K. S. Stanislavskogo*. [The life and work of K. S. Stanislavsky, 4 volumes]. Moscow Art Theatre Press.

CHAPTER 6

Conclusion

Abstract The Conclusion summaries the main findings emerging from the book. It highlights the malleability of improvisation as a practice that can be adapted to a range of rehearsal and performance situations. The book ends with a number of historiographical and research perspectives aimed at facilitating similar works. These perspectives take the form of advice about: (i) choosing a research focus (ii) structuring one's narrative (iii) finding a balance between primary and secondary sources (iv) positioning a book within a one's larger research trajectory.

Keywords Improvisation · Research methods · Academic training · Autoethnography

On paper, Active Analysis seems very simple.[1] Actors read a scene, discuss it briefly, and then start improvising on their feet their own interpretation of the Given Circumstances. Further improvisations then move progressively towards the actual words of the text. The reality of doing, however, is of course much more complex. Active Analysis is a holistic approach that allows actors to tap into their emotional, physical, and rational reservoirs, depending on their ever-changing needs or their own 'here, today, now'. It also allows them the possibility of analysing a text while searching at the same time for the means of embodying it. In placing improvisation as the beating heart of such a dynamic approach as Active Analysis, Stanislavsky was essentially underscoring the potential which improvisation has in meeting the actor's diverse needs in training, rehearsal, and performance; he was also placing improvisation as a means that bridges together these various facets of the actor's work. In Active Analysis, actors become the authors of their actions, interpretations, and characters, with improvisation acting as their main tool.

In an often-quoted letter to his son, Stanislavsky referred to the work that he was doing in the mid-to-late 1930s as 'a *new* device [...] a *new* approach to the role. It involves reading the play today, and tomorrow rehearsing it on stage' (quoted in Carnicke, 2009: 194; emphasis added—note that Stanislavsky did not use the words 'Active Analysis', as these were later coined by Knebel). More than a new discovery, recent scholarship prefers to foreground a sense of continuity (Shevtsova, 2023) or accumulation (Aquilina, 2012a) in Stanislavsky's development as a theatre-maker as he moved resolutely towards his final legacies. Within this trajectory, improvisation played a key role, even if in his vision and as evidenced here, Stanislavsky's use of improvisation was not bound to one particular interpretation, definition, or application. Certainly, improvisation will always concern itself with the present moment in the actor's work, with the here and now; it values aliveness and an organic engagement with the role. Beyond that, however, Stanislavsky's use of improvisation was a dynamic one, which is another way of saying that it answered to his own specific work situations, to his own present moment. Over the course of a long career spanning some fifty years, 'improvisation' served as a term to signpost a range of qualities, aspects of work, and acting or production techniques. At various points in Stanislavsky's career improvisation was: a way for the actor to carve creative independence from the text, the type, and the director; a rehearsal technique to find character nuance; a training approach to develop technical skills; an attempt to write theatre scripts; and an approach to create the mise-en-scène. It was also variously linked to the everyday life of the actor and to the collective ensemble. In Stanislavsky's work improvisation ranged from fixing an unexpected 'mistake' on stage to seeing improvisation in a close and enabling relationship with structure; he also spoke about developing an inner state of improvisation that is unique to every performance, to experiencing the role anew every night. Stanislavsky's use of improvisation was therefore an expanded one, allowing it to be applied today

6 CONCLUSION

in thoroughly unique work circumstances which he could have hardly imagined.

To conclude, I would like to shift the discussion and share some historiographical and research perspectives emerging from the writing of this book. These perspectives are informed by my own desire to reflect on *how* I carry out my work and to understand my own processes in view of becoming a better researcher—a direct spin-off of Stanislavsky's own 'work upon the self'. In my eyes, research has many similarities with improvisation. We often start a research project with a particular set of objectives and questions, which we then feel the need to fine-tune or even change altogether once we encounter the material. We go in the archives or in the field hoping to find some specific material, but then come across something altogether different. What are we going to do? Are we going to discard this new material, or improvise ways of bringing it into our research? Improvisation in the actor's work is initiated when the actor encounters the creative material, be it an image, piece of text, stage partner, a structure of actions, a set of instructions, a series of given circumstances, etc. In this encounter the actor is never a neutral being but they try to make sense of the material by actively bringing in their own experiences, emotions, ideas, and personal attributes. I see the work of the researcher on similar lines. I will always remind fellow researchers of the importance of a strong, objective methodology (the structure in the actor's work or line of physical actions), but this should not come at the price of subjectivity (the unique inner state of improvisation which Merlin speaks about). Like the actor, the researcher is a very real human being with their own ideological views, intentions, skills, and backgrounds which they use to navigate the research material, fashioning it in turn into a plausible and polished outcome. The way an actor improvises can therefore tell us a lot about how we carry out our research, not only in theatre and performance but also beyond to effectively expand the influence of our disciplines.

The research perspectives that I offer below are also meant as a series of pointers aimed at facilitating further studies. I think we all have at one point or another experienced a block in our scholarly work, such as trying to find sources, organising the material, articulating ideas, or presenting them in written form. (Actors are also certainly familiar with their own set of blocks, including when improvising.) The perspectives offered here can hopefully help scholars engaged in similar projects to overcome such blocks. Based as they are on my own experience as a writer and researcher, this last part of the book can therefore be seen to contain traces of autoethnographic writing.[2] Autoethnography is a research methodology rooted in a researcher's own experience and the insight that this generates in the study of a particular issue, theme, practice, or reality. It values the subjective engagement of the researcher with their area of study, in a way that contrasts with more scientific approaches to research that foreground detachment and objectivity. In the narrative that I developed above about Stanislavsky's use of improvisation I tried to be as objective as possible, as required by historical research, but in this last part I purposely shift tone and embrace my own subjectivity as a researcher. Far from a mere indulgence on the part of the researcher, such autoethnographic accounts do not simply narrate the researcher's experience but, crucially, they also connect with broader discourses taking place in the field. In other words, autoethnographic writings provide a personalised perspective on an issue that is of significance to a wider community (Adams et al., 2015: 27). In my case, the issue at hand revolves around a concern with the '*how?*' question: how does one carry out (historical) research in theatre and performance? Autoethnographical projects are typically concerned with serious and even difficult realities, such as social injustice, coming out, bodily stigma, racial inequalities, and so on. As Holman Jones et al. (2013: 32) write that autoethnographic writings '[manoeuvre] through pain, confusion, anger, and uncertainty and making life better'. Studying past events and historical figures is not expected to be traumatic (though it could be), but neither is it inconsequential. In fact, the wider community I am engaging with comprises the scholarly community that like me tries to make sense of the past in the belief that a knowledge of that past can help us understand the present and even prepare for the future. It is this broader community of researchers that I address here with these perspectives.

1. *Choosing a focus.* Why did I choose to focus on improvisation? How did I come to this topic? A number of circumstances were at play. In a first instance, my decision to work on improvisation was dictated by the fact that I could not see any other source that attempts such a career-wide survey of its use by Stanislavsky. Certainly, improvisation features in most books on Stanislavsky, but my study firmly places improvisation at its core and makes it its subject matter. This allows me to make the all-important claim in academia that my work is 'original' and that it makes a 'valuable contribution to knowledge'. This contribution to knowledge

manifests itself in two ways, namely (i) in the content of the book (by referring to side-lined realities in Stanislavsky's work that literature has never tackled in any depth) and (ii) in the presentation (or organisation) of the material in four distinct phases (more on this below). Scholars, especially early career ones, can at times be anxious about finding their place within established scholarly fields that have an extensive history and very clear scholarly milestones – Stanislavsky is certainly a case in point. My advice here is to remember that originality can take various forms. It can certainly be evidenced in the content or presentation of your work, as was the case here (and complex realities like Stanislavsky will always have untapped areas to get into); however, originality can also be found in the perspective that is brought in to drive the study, what is sometimes referred to as 'framing'. For example, see the invitation which Jonathan Pitches poses to Meyerhold scholars but which can easily be generalised and related to wider research endeavours:

> Thinking more broadly [than the short appraisal of Meyerhold's work with female theatre-makers that is offered], I hope this example might prompt a whole series of re-readings of [his work], ones based on theoretical foundations which have come to prominence in theatre studies since 1969. Some examples might include: Meyerhold and material culture, Meyerhold and audience research, Meyerhold and theories of immersion, Meyerhold and documentation, Meyerhold and cultural transmission, Meyerhold and inter-culturalism. (Pitches, 2016: 13)

The application of cultural and critical theories can certainly do much to offer fresh insights into well-trodden research areas. It is a methodology that served me well a number of times, particularly when reading Russian theatre through the theories of everyday life (Aquilina, 2012b, 2012c, 2013, 2018) and cultural transmission (Aquilina, 2019 and 2020). The application of theory also allows historical or practice-based research to connect with the more 'theoretical' nature of academia, and to forge links with scholars outside of theatre and performance who also use critical theory in their work. These links are also important for funding purposes to underline the interdisciplinary or cross-disciplinary nature of a project.

The flipside of having a focus is that it can become an all-constraining framework that binds rather than informs the study. This is the very real risk where sources or material collected are made to fit within the focus, whereas a critical attitude is more helpful to discern the material and separate what is really relevant from what is not. Remember that Stanislavsky himself discarded what he felt was superfluous in the improvisations of the actors: the same discerning attitude is necessary when going through the sources. Any discarded material is never really dispensed with, as it is often recollected in the most unexpected places to inform other projects—a feeling which actors are also familiar with. Such material typically rests at the back of your mind. When working on this book it was clear that some material was more pertinent than other, and that huge chunks of work in Stanislavsky's career could never fit in the narrative that I was developing. Simply put, they needed to be omitted. This is an example of the critical and discerning attitude that led to the choice of some examples and phases over others. In short, a focus is there to help you discern, analyse, frame, and organise the material—don't let it become your horse blinder.

2. *Structuring the narrative.* My identification of four phases in Stanislavsky's work was a subjective choice, but not an arbitrary one. I came to it after serious engagement with the sources over a prolonged period of time. Stanislavsky remains, after all, my main area of research. An overtly fastidious reader might say that in focusing on these four phases I have only created gaps in the narrative, and that I was not exhaustive enough in what I covered. I always felt that such reactions are driven by a misguided attitude that is concerned by what is *missing* in a work rather than valuing what is *present*. I don't believe that anyone can ever be exhaustive when undertaking historical or even some other study in theatre and performance, especially when new sources come to light, or when our own research methods are continuously updated. Therefore, aim for the rigorous collection and analysis of sources to create supported narratives, but in the full knowledge that closure is never realistic.

In any case, my structuring of the narrative in four phases helped me to make sense of the material which, related as it was to a key figure in modern theatre, was indeed comprehensive. Any gaps in the narrative are also an invitation for further research arising from this study, which I hope other scholars will take on board. Taking research cues from others is, after all, one way for any discipline to grow.

3. *A balance between primary and secondary sources.* The use of primary sources when discussing a theatre-maker like Stanislavsky remains essential to unlock his work. However, secondary sources are also a necessary

part of the research process. They might help you to contextualise primary sources, support your analysis, or even identify research gaps. For example, all my work on *Artists and Admirers* (3 essays and a section in a monograph, not to mentioned the piece above) was triggered by the following one sentence in Jean Benedetti's book: 'Thus neither *Dead Souls*, which opened on December 9, 1932, after two years' work, nor Ostrovski's *Artists and Admirers* which opened on September 23, 1933, corresponded entirely to his wishes' (Benedetti, 1999: 342). This sentence made me think: 'Wow! This is a production which I never heard of before and which we seem to know little about!' Therefore, inspiration for research projects (or even for improvisatory work) can be found anywhere, so do keep your eyes open!

This time round, I started working on each phase by consulting the secondary sources first, books like Benedetti's *Stanislavski: His Life and Art* and to a lesser extent Maria Shevtsova's *Rediscovering Stanislavsky*. This was a hunch I had that, given the length of Stanislavsky's career, I might be better served by initially reading a summary of his work, one that would lead me on to specific moments of his career that demanded further study. Primary sources like his Collected Works and Koonen's and Knebel's autobiographies then came into the picture. Irina Vinogradskia's monumental *Zhizn i tvorchestvo K. S. Stanislavskogo* [The Life and Work of K. S. Stanislavsky] was another essential source, particularly because it drew my attention to some other primary sources. In any case, I would suggest the flexibility that drives improvisation as a model to adopt when reading your primary and secondary sources: some projects, like this on here, benefit from reading the secondary sources first; other projects require an immediate engagement with primary material, while yet other projects might benefit from a close juxtaposition of the two.

Any scholarly work needs to converse with current literature and debates taking place in your field. Book proposals even ask you to be upfront in how your work connects with other examples in the field. The connection with other sources is even more important when undertaking doctoral research, where it is often placed as one of the assessment criteria. All this makes the choice of secondary sources a particularly important one, and researchers are always encouraged to look at sources that are recent, that critique the subject, and which are recognised among peers. On the other hand, in my use here of primary sources I have at times opted to quote at some length, especially when these sources are unavailable in English translation. My hope is that these long quotations could be helpful to other scholars engaged in their own research.

4. *Positioning the book within a larger research trajectory.* I also arrived at the topic of improvisation in a rather tangential manner. I was working on another, rather different project, an autoethnographic study of how academics carry out, or perform, their work. (Surely it is no coincidence that I am concluding this short book with some personal writing!) This other study, a full-length monograph, included a chapter on community engagement, in which I discuss several workshops I carried out with different theatre communities. These workshops carried a particular research question, namely how improvisation can be adapted to answer the training needs of different groups. To prepare myself for these workshops I read as much as I could on improvisation, and this reading invariably led me to Stanislavsky. I was carrying out this larger research during a year-long sabbatical, when circumstances dictated a change of focus into a different, more contained project. I had gone through so many sources on improvisation and Stanislavsky that it seemed logical for me to focus my last sabbatical months on that.

I am recounting this experience to underline the fact that very few research projects are self-contained units. From my experience, research leads to other research, and when an open mind is kept, new opportunities tend to present themselves. Different research projects connect with one another, as was the case here: it was the larger project about academic performance that led me to this smaller project on Stanislavsky and improvisation. There was also a degree of overlap between the two, but I do not see this overlap as a negative thing. It rather means that the research that I was doing in improvisation, and the awareness emerging from it, fed into two different research outputs. Certainly no material was repeated between the two but, on the other hand, the two projects supported each other, helping me to maximise on sources, time, and my overall research and work. And now that I am finishing this book and returning to the larger volume my understanding is certainly enriched by the very focused work that I carried out here.

My advice to young scholars is to consider how one's research plans balance between the creation of short-term outputs (typically universities ask for one or two research outputs like a journal article every year) and longer and more substantial projects. The latter, like a book, are very helpful in the context of promotion when you need to demonstrate expertise in the field. However, do not see these outputs in isolation, or else you would need to restart from scratch every time you start a new project. Think rather in terms of continuity, in the same way that Stanislavsky's career developed over fifty years and, while he certainly evidenced clear milestones along the way, an element of work like improvisation recurred in different places and in different forms. Keeping a 'research diary' can also be helpful, not only to record the work carried out, but also to jot down ideas as they come to you. These may include connections between projects or ideas for further research. In my experience, these ideas often come to you when working on some other task, during discussions with colleagues, work with students, or even in unexpected moments of the day.

Research is meant to be a joyful experience, an opportunity to pursue what you are really passionate about. It might not be an easy ride, but the rewards can be substantial, both professionally and, from my experience, personally. Create your structures, connect with partners and colleagues in your field, trust your 'here, today, now', lay down the necessary ground work and, ultimately, perform and improvise your way throughout the process!

Notes

1. Among Stanislavsky's many discoveries and approaches, it is Active Analysis that now seems to hold our attention the most, in terms of both scholarship and practice. Consequently, literature about Active Analysis abounds and is increasing, which is why I do not go into further detail on it to focus on other things. The following are only some examples of current literature on Active Analysis: Chambers (2024), Arp-Dunham (2024), Shevtsova (2023), Blair (2014), Merlin (2023 and 2014), Carnicke (2023), Knebel (2022), and Thomas (2016).
2. Valuable introductions to autoethnography as a research methodology include Adams et al. (2015), Poulus (2021), and Chang et al. (2013).

References

Adams, T. E., Holman Jones, S., & Ellis, C. (Eds.). (2015). *Autoethnography*. Oxford University Press.
Aquilina, S. (2012a). Stanislavski's accumulative practice in *Artists and Admirers* rehearsals (1932–33). *Stanislavski Studies*, 2, 3–20.
Aquilina, S. (2012b). Stanislavski's encounter with the Revolution. *Studies in Theatre and Performance*, 32(1), 79–91.
Aquilina, S. (2012c). Stanislavsky and the impact of studio ethics on everyday life. *Theatre, Dance and Performance Training*, 3(3), 302–14.
Aquilina, S. (2013). Stanislavski and the tactical potential of everyday images. *Theatre Research International*, 38(3), 229–39.
Aquilina, S. (2018). Meyerhold and the revolution: A reading through Henri Lefebvre's theories on "everyday life." *Theatre History Studies*, 37, 3–26.
Aquilina, S. (2019). Cultural transmission of actor training techniques: A research project. *Theatre, Dance and Performance Training*, 10(1), 4–20.
Aquilina, S. (2020). *Modern theatre in Russia: Tradition building and transmission processes*. Bloomsbury.
Arp-Dunham, J. R. (2024). Active Analysis for beginning acting students: A class blueprint. *Stanislavski Studies*, 12(1), 87–108.
Benedetti, J. (1999). *Stanislavski: His life and art*. Methuen.
Blair, R. (2014). Active Analysis—more active than you know: Stanislavsky and cognitive science. In A. White (Ed.), *The Routledge companion to Stanislavsky* (pp. 308–20). Routledge.
Carnicke, S. (2009). *Stanislavsky in focus* (2nd ed.). Routledge.
Carnicke, S. (2023). *Dynamic acting through Active Analysis*. Bloomsbury Publishing.
Chambers, D. (2024). *Analysis through action for actors and directors: From Stanislavskt to contemporary performance*. Routledge.
Chang, H., Ngunjiri, F. W., & Hernandez, K. C. (2013). *Collaborative autoethnography*. Routledge.
Jones, H., Adams, T., & Ellis, C. (Eds.). (2013). *Handbook of autoethnography*. Routledge.
Knebel, M. (2022). *Active Analysis*, (A. Vassiliev, Ed., I. Brown, Trans.). Routledge.
Merlin, B. (2014). "Here, today, now": Active Analysis for the twenty-first-century actor. In A. White (Ed.), *The routledge companion to Stanislavsky* (pp. 325–40). Routledge.
Merlin, B. (2023). Hear, now, today: Active Analysis for the working actor a "special guest workshop" delivered at the S Word, Prague, 12 November 2022. *Stanislavski Studies*, 11(1), 81–98.
Pitches, J. (2016). Introduction. In E. Braun (Ed.), *Meyerhold on theatre* (4th ed., pp. 1–18). Methuen.

Poulos, C. N. (2021). *Essentials of autoethnography*. American Psychological Association.
Shevtsova, M. (2023). "Music, singing, word, action": The Opera-Dramatic Studio 1935–1938. *Stanislavski Studies, 11*(1), 3–18.
Thomas, J. (2016). *A director's guide to Stanislavsky's Active Analysis: including the formative essay on Active Analysis by Maria Knebel*. Bloomsbury.

Index

A
A Burning Heart, 57, 65
action, 18, 22, 23, 38–40, 45, 46, 54, 56, 57, 59, 60, 62, 70, 71
active analysis, 3, 25, 32, 54, 58, 59, 63, 64, 69, 70, 77
adaptation, 40
Aeschylus, 57
affective memory, 41. *See also* emotion memory
Aikhenvald, Yury, 42
Alekseev Circle, 13, 15, 28
Alexandrinsky Theatre, 23
amateur years, 3
An Actor's Work, 1, 10, 40
Andreev, Leonid, 20
  The Life of Man, 19, 20
An Enemy of the People, 19, 61
animal improvisations, 41
Artists and Admirers, 3, 60–63, 75
attention, 9–11, 32, 37, 40, 45, 49, 65, 75, 77
autoethnography, 72

B
belief, 37, 40, 72
Birman, Serafima, 36
Boleslavsky, Richard, 36
Bolshevik Party, 54

C
characterisation/character/character work, 9, 10, 12, 13, 18, 20–29, 39, 43, 46, 47, 56–58, 62, 63, 70
Chekhov, Anton, 18, 24, 25
  The Cherry Orchard, 18, 24, 26
  The Seagull, 18, 24, 66
  Three Sisters, 60
Chekhov, Michael, 36, 44, 50, 51, 58
Chernov, 8, 14
Chirikov, E., 26, 32
  Ivan Mironich, 26, 27, 32
Chronegk, Ludwig, 18
circles of attention, 39
collective work/collectivity/communal work, 48
communication, 40

concentration, 36, 39
constant state of inner improvisation, 46
COVID-19, 4
crowd scenes, 19, 50, 55, 58, 59

D
demonstrations, 20, 22, 23, 55
devised theatre, 48
directing, 3, 18
director-dictator, 18
Duse, Eleonora, 10

E
emotion, 36, 39, 46, 69, 71
emotion memory, 40. *See also* affective memory
emploi, 11. *See also* type
ensemble, 39, 70
étude, 25, 32, 38, 39, 48
everyday life, 12, 20, 24, 27, 28, 48, 70, 73
Evreinov, Nikolai, 42

F
final legacies, 3, 54, 70
First Studio, 3, 27, 29, 36–42, 44, 49, 50
flow, 59, 61, 66
fragmentation, 36, 61

G
gestures, 8, 10–12, 31, 45, 47, 50, 59, 61
Ghosts, 19, 21, 22, 31
given circumstances, 32, 63, 69, 71
Gorchakov, Nikolai, 15, 55
Gorky, Maxim, 21, 23, 39, 42, 43
Children of the Sun, 19, 23

Gorky's method, 39, 42, 59
Grotowski, Jerzy, 44

H
Hamsun, Knut, 20
The Drama of Life, 19, 20
here, today, now, 3, 4, 63, 69, 77
hybridity, 38

I
Ibsen, Henrik, 31
An Enemy of the People, 18
Ghosts, 19
imagination, 18, 25, 27, 32, 42, 45, 48, 67
imperial theatres, 8
interpretation, 3, 10, 37, 50, 56, 57, 63, 66, 69, 70
Ivan Mironich, 3, 26, 27

J
justification, 40

K
Kachalov, Vasily, 22, 23
Kerensky, Alexander, 54
Kerzhentsev, Platon, 38
Kiselevsky, Ivan, 11, 12
Knebel, Maria, 58–61, 64, 67, 70, 75, 77
Knipper, Olga, 22, 26, 31, 36
Komissarzhevsky, Fyodor, 42
Koonen, Alisa, 19, 23, 29, 75
Korsh, 11
Kotliarevskaia, Vera, 23, 24

L
laboratory, 36, 49

Lensky, Aleksandr, 8
Les Merchands de Gloire, 57, 65, 66
Litovtseva, N.N., 23, 60
logic, 29, 46, 60
Lunacharsky, Anatoly, 57, 66
Luzhsky, Vasily, 26
Lvov, Georgy, 54

M
Maeterlinck, Maurice, 20, 32
  The Blue Bird, 19, 20
Maly Theatre, 7, 12
mannerisms, 7, 9, 13, 28
Markov, Pavel, 49, 50, 54
Meinengen, 18
Melania, Olga, 23
method of physical action, 46
Meyerhold, Vsevolod, 21, 73
micro scene, 9, 47
mise-en-scène, 18, 20, 27, 46, 58–60, 62, 66, 70. See also production plan
mood, 18, 45
Morozov, Savva, 21
Moscow Art Theatre, 15, 18, 49, 54, 60
Moscow Proletkult, 48
muscular release, 40
Musil, Nikolai, 7–9, 11

N
Nemirovich-Danchenko, Vladimir, 20–22, 29, 42, 43, 54, 60
Nicholas I and the Decembrists, 58

O
object, 9, 39
objective, 40, 56, 59, 71, 72
opera, 14, 54
Opera-Dramatic Studio, 58

Ostrovsky, Aleksandr, 9, 57, 60, 66
  A Burning Heart, 57
  Artists and Admirers, 60
  The Marriage of Balzaminov, 9
Ouspenskaya, Maria, 36

P
production plan, 18, 19, 21, 22, 26.
  See also mise-en-scène

R
rehearsal, 2–4, 12, 13, 15, 18, 20–24, 26, 27, 32, 36, 41, 43, 46–48, 50, 55–58, 60–64, 66, 70
research methods, 74
rhythm, 39, 41, 55, 56, 63
Richards, Thomas, 44

S
Sadovski, Prov, 8, 14
Savitskaya, Margarita, 22
score, 9, 18, 46, 61
Second Studio, 49, 54, 58
Society of Arts and Literature, 17
spectators/spectatorship/audience, 2, 10–12, 14, 18, 19, 22, 25, 32, 46, 47, 57, 60, 61, 65, 73
spontaneity/spontaneous, 2, 10, 12, 22, 44, 46, 61, 62
Stalin, Joseph, 56
Stanislavsky System, 55
structure, 39, 44, 45, 59, 60, 62, 70, 71, 77
subtext, 40, 45, 60
Sudakov, Ilya, 54, 60
Sulerzhitsky, Leopold, 21, 36
symbolism/symbolist plays, 20

T
technique/technical work, 8, 9, 19, 20, 25, 26, 36, 41, 46, 47, 50, 62, 70
text analysis, 38
theatre histories/historiography/history-based research/historical research, 2–4, 72
Theatre-Studio, 21
The Blue Bird, 19, 20, 32, 36
The Cherry Orchard, 18, 24
The Drama of Life, 19–21, 23
The Life of Man, 19, 20
The Marriage of Balzaminov, 9
The Marriage of Figaro, 56, 65, 66
The Seagull, 18, 24
throughaction, 36, 56, 65
Tolstoy, Aleksei, 43
training, 4, 8, 29, 39, 41, 49, 50, 70, 76

truth, 28, 37, 40, 50
type, 11, 15, 25, 27, 70. *See also* emploi

V
Vakhtangov, Yevgeny, 36–38, 46–51, 60
Vasiliev, Anatoly, 38
Verhaeren, Émile, 48
Vershilov, B.I., 63

W
Woe from Wit, 19, 55, 56
work upon the self, 71

Z
Zon, Boris, 62

GPSR Compliance

The European Union's (EU) General Product Safety Regulation (GPSR) is a set of rules that requires consumer products to be safe and our obligations to ensure this.

If you have any concerns about our products, you can contact us on ProductSafety@springernature.com

In case Publisher is established outside the EU, the EU authorized representative is:

Springer Nature Customer Service Center GmbH
Europaplatz 3
69115 Heidelberg, Germany

Batch number: 08386912

Printed by Printforce, the Netherlands